INDIANA AT RANDOM
... ON ROADS LESS TRAVELED

D1198444

By Wendell Trogdon

JOURNEYS ON THE SLOW LANES

Published in the United States

Backroads Press
P.O. Box 651
Mooresville IN 46158

ISBN 0-9642371-9-9

Cover by Gary Varvel

Pictures by Fabian Trogdon

Maps from Indiana Department of Transportation

Printed by Country Pines, Inc.
Shoals, Indiana

CONTENTS

DEDICATION

To Travis, Kayla, Maggie and Wesley, our four grandchildren. May their endless quest for knowledge lead them down roads lined with spectacular scenery, panoramic vistas and an appreciation of the Master's creation.

BACKGROUND

Interstates are built for speed, quick routes to a destination, the drives soon forgotten. Roads less traveled are more intimate. Those who drive them can enjoy the scenery, feel a part of the places they stop, and find the state's hidden treasures too few Hoosiers see.

We drove 15 of those highways, stopping at each of the 200 towns and cities along the way. Some of the roads stretch across the state from south to north, some from east to west. A few are shorter routes through unsullied beauty.

We found each mile different. And each road memorable.

BEST TOWNS

BEST CITIES

(Based on the roads traveled)

Oldenburg	Bluffton
Corydon	Greensburg
Montpelier	Delphi
Farmland	Batesville
Fairmount	
Flora	**BEST KEPT SECRETS**
Brookville	Merom
Nashville	Montpelier
Hope	Oldenburg
Lagrange	Albiong
Bluffton	Odon
Salem	Vallonia

SCENES TO REMEMBER

Ind. 1 - Between Greendale and St. Leon.

Ind. 450 - From Bedford to Shoals.

Ind. 46 - Southeast in fall toward Spencer.

Ind. 58 - Merom Overlook.

Ind. 135 - Atop a ridge south of Salem.

OVERVIEW

We are the roads we take, the stops we make along the way, the people we meet, the areas we visit, the memorials we see, the history we relive.

We are a part of yesterday, a slice of today. If we are fortunate, we leave a bit of what we learn along the way for tomorrow.

Roads are the sound tracks of our lives. The crinkle of maps stirs a wanderlust within us. Rubber on pavement whets our anticipation of what is ahead. Noise of cities summons us to their streets. The stillness of tiny towns challenges us, it seems, to uncover their secrets.

Sounds of combines in fields return us to the days of our youth. Chatter around liars' tables at small restaurants remind us of the camaraderie of the small towns we once knew.

*   *   *

Life itself, as Norman Mailer observed, has taken on the character of the interstates. It once took us twice as long to get from one town to another, but the drive was interesting. It seemed intimate, and we felt like we were a part of each mile along the way.

That experience can be relived on many Indiana roads. We traveled 15 of those highways for this book we choose to call *Indiana At Random . . . On Roads Less Traveled*. In it, we share with you the observations we made through areas of the state too often overlooked by those who travel the four-lane interstates.

Some of the roads rise and fall, turn and twist, meander and wander. Vistas open to panoramic splendor. Small towns appear around curves, then straggle up hills where homes are anchored on slopes.

Other routes are straight and true, entering cities and towns on narrow streets, many of which are still free of urban sprawl.

Other roads pass through the prairies of west central Indiana where corn and soybeans thrive in soil dark and rich. Huge grain storage bins rise toward cloudless skies, free of pollution.

On east near Ohio, remnants of sloughs remain among reclaimed land.

Markers along the way are tributes to white men who negotiated treaties with Indians . . . and for Indian chiefs who won concessions from white men.

To the south, beef herds graze on rolling slopes lush with grass after heavy rains. Elsewhere, the hills are more severe, the cliffs deep.

Pheasants can be seen on Ind. 18 in Benton County, wild turkeys on Ind. 135 in Brown County, deer on Ind. 446 in Monroe County.

Natural lakes dot the terrain in northeast Indiana; ponds formed in depressions to the south. Along the way are dams that provide recreational opportunities and help control flooding.

Roads Less Traveled cut through towns, passing courthouses that are majestic reminders of an era when architecture was more than straight lines void of form as seen in box stores near interchanges.

Each of the 15 roads is reviewed in detail, described as we observed them. We have attempted to evaluate each route as accurately as possible, but we are Hoosiers who search for the positive and may at times overlook the negative.

We have pinpointed most of the attractions on the road. Some of the restaurants we liked are mentioned. You likely will find your own fascinations and prefer other diners for leisurely travel is a time to discover the new.

If you enjoy the freedom of roads less traveled you likely will share our enthusiasm. We wish you 15 delightful journeys.

INDIANA 450

BEDFORD TO SHOALS
Panorama of Nature

History and scenery line Ind. 450 as it winds its way between Bedford and U.S. 50 west of Shoals.

History can be found at Williams on the banks of White River and at Trinity Springs and Indian Springs, two towns now only ghosts of a more notable past.

One scenic view follows another on much of the 25-mile drive that is gently rolling at times, sharply hilly on occasions.

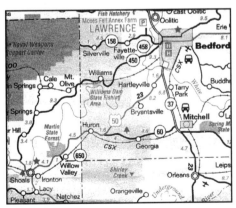

In the fall, the leaves cast a pallet of reds, crimsons, yellows and siennas on the wooded hills. It is a panorama of nature unequaled by Brown County . . . and free of the traffic that crowds the roads to Nashville each autumn.

The drive on Ind. 450 from Bedford southwest is more spectacular, but it is recommended that the road be observed in both directions to view the panoramas that open in each direction.

And it is a route worth taking regardless of the season of the year.

Ind. 450 begins a half-mile west of Ind. 37 off Ind. 158 at Bedford's west edge, passes through a residential area called Bex Addition, then begins its continual twists and turns to the southwest. The town of Williams is nine miles ahead.

In a river bottom a mile or so ahead, the road crosses an embankment, protected with guard rail. Ahead, a farmer mows weeds along a fence row, his pride in his property obvious.

The road deviates at times, its sharp turns approaching 90-degree angles. A Church of Christ is built into the hill. Not far away on another sharp turn is a huge house that looks as if it belongs on an estate, its three-car garage attached, its lawn attractively landscaped with shrubs.

A smaller house next door is being remodeled in what may be a "keeping up with neighbors" syndrome.

Near Williams, the road runs under a railroad trestle, its clearance 12 feet 11 inches. Dead ahead, except for a curve in the road, is the backwaters of the East Fork of White River.

WILLIAMS

A Dam Site

At the edge of Williams, the Spice Valley Recreation area is between the river and the road. In town, past the "Welcome to Williams" sign, Ind. 450 crosses the railroad, which separates the river from the town, much of which is anchored on the side of the steep hill.

Half way up the incline is Pinnick's Country Store; "ice cream, sundaes, shakes, banana splits, cones," a sign on the door notes. Pinnick's, however, is more than that. It's a place for Hoosier Hospitality, a gathering spot for the community, a return to the general stores of an earlier era.

Another business across the street has night crawlers, $1 a dozen, for it is the river that is a source of income for some residents. Atop the hill is the old Williams High School, a victim of school consolidation. It now houses apartments for renters.

The Williams post offices is across the street in a brick building.

Back down the hill, the Williams Milling Company no longer stores grain or turns wheat into flour as it did in the mid-1900s when the late Leland Williams operated it as he did for four decades. The mill sits idle.

White River flows over Williams Dam

A few feet away are trash bins for use by Lawrence County residents. A sign reads, "No Martin County trash." One neighbor's trash is not necessarily another's treasure.

In the river is Williams Dam, once the source of electric power for a vast area, now a public fishing area operated by the state Division of Fish and Wildlife. Visitors to the dam are warned to use caution for the water is hazardous and dangerous.

A bronze marker in memory of conservation officer First Sgt. Karl Kelley is not far from the dam. Kelley lost his life April 17, 1988, while saving the lives of his fellow officers. "People like you are few and far between," the tribute to Kelley reads.

The tragedy occurred when Kelley and other conservation officers were practicing how to conduct a rescue in the rampaging river which was six feet above normal at the time.

An overlook with a park-like setting is a few hundred feet down stream.

As it leaves Williams, Ind. 450 passes Hammersley Lane, which seems appropriate for Stella Hammersley is one of the town's more noted residents and author of the book, *Williams: White River Memories.*

*   *   *

A county road leads off Ind. 450 a short distance to the south to one of the state's famed covered bridges. It stretches 358 feet over White River, making it one of the longest bridges still in use in the state. It remains—as it has since 1884—a vital link from Williams south to U.S. 50 and Huron.

West of Williams, limbs of trees reach out from each side of the road turning the road into nature's tunnel as the pavement rises above the White River bottoms. Atop the rise is Mt. Olive Church of Christ, a fixture since 1870. A cemetery is on the grounds.

Lawrence County ends, Martin County begins. Curves cause speeds to drop, but it is of no concern. There is little traffic and no reason to rush. Much of the road is lined with trees, except for an open area north of Trinity Springs.

TRINITY SPRINGS

Curative Waters

Trinity Springs' past exceeds its present. Only about twenty homes and two churches—Baptist and Church of Christ—are in the town marked by four 90-degree turns. There is no industry and no business outlets.

It is a far different place than it was in the first three decades of the 1900s. That was an era when Americans were fascinated by mineral water and hotels with spas attracted the wealthy. Martin County's sulphur springs were first discovered in the mid-1800s, but the spas did not become popular until railroads were built and transportation made travel easier.

Sign at north entrance to Trinity Springs

Both Trinity Springs and Indian Springs would become destinations after World War I for those who sought the magic cures the water was said to offer.

Some locals were not impressed. "Stinking water," they called the sulphur.

Trinity Springs, platted in 1848, called itself, "Martin County's famous health and pleasure resort" and boasted of hotels such as the Pines, the Lundy, the Akle's, the Ballad and Reid's, and, of course, the Trinity Springs. The hotels rented rooms for $1 to $2 a day. Liveries had horses for those who chose to ride or tour the area in carriages or buggies.

Boom times do not last. They did not for Trinity Springs. War and the automobile changed America and it did Trinity Springs as it did Indian Springs. Few clues remain of the fame that was once Trinity Springs. Its high school closed in 1943, a lack of students, and of teachers, the reason.

INDIAN SPRINGS

"Wild and Romantic"

A short distance west from Trinity Springs, narrow, twisting Martin County Road 81 leads north through swamps and woodlands two miles to Indian Springs.

A one-lane bridge takes traffic high over Indian Creek. A "No Trespassing" sign is at road side, an unfortunate deterrent for the wet land appears ideal for mushrooms on this warm spring weekday.

Indian Springs has 20 or so houses, most of which are scattered along the railroad. Overalls dry on a line outside one home for this is now a working community; its days of leisurely baths in mineral waters are buried in the past.

A concrete business building is marked as Indian Creek Hills Inc. It is closed.

Still impressive, despite its age, is a huge square house, its metal roof rising to a peak from all four sides. Now a home, it was, we learn later, the Dobson Hotel which continued to accept guests until 1940.

When Indian Springs was a thriving community, the hotels boasted of its ideal location on the Evansville and Richmond Railroad and its connection with trains at Washington, Elnora, Bedford and Seymour. "The most accessible summer resort in the state," the advertisements claimed and added its springs were:

"Situated in the wild, romantic and highly picturesque mineral region of Indiana."

Among the fixtures at the time were Dillon's General Store and Inman's Store.

In his book, *Photographic History of Martin County*, Bill Whorrall explains: "Autos came and guests no longer had to remain at a hotel for a week or more. The pace of life sped up and left the grand old hotels behind. Now, the public went to tourists spots, saw the attractions and went home. If home was too far away they stopped at tourists cabins along the highway."

*   *   *

We return to Ind. 450 and continue southwest. The road passes the first sizable farm fields we have seen since Williams. Tile silos remain at a barn that is void of some of its siding, a fading reminder of a time when farms were small and each had its own character. Across the road is a rusting threshing machine replaced by combines six decades earlier.

DOVER HILL

Turning the Corners

Again the road winds and the speed drops as we enter Dover Hill past the 1890 Methodist Church and the Dover Hill Christian Union Church.

It's impossible to speed through Dover Hill for there are nine—yes, nine—90-degree turns to negotiate. The slow pace allows motorists to appreciate the neat homes with trimmed lawns.

Dover Hill, too, has had its good times and bad. Established in 1846, it was known at times as Harrisonville, at times as Doverhill before again becoming Dover Hill.

It was the Martin County seat of government for a short time before the Civil War when its future seemed bright. Dreams for continued growth were shattered when the railroad was routed to the south through Shoals, which would become the county seat.

Dover Hill is now a residential community, its only business along the road a Perdue poultry farm at the south edge of town.

                    *   *   *

More abandoned farm buildings are off Ind. 450 south of Dover Hill. A "Good Luck Rox" sign for the Shoals High School athletic teams (the Jug Rox) is off the road.

At Martin County Road 1326, the Friendship United Methodist Church, a small frame building with limited parking on crushed stone, is at the edge of the road. Visitors are greeted at the door by a "Come—Let Us Go Into The House Of The Lord" sign. A note on an oak tree reveals the Hickory Ridge Cemetery Association is seeking donations for upkeep and care of the adjoining cemetery. "All donations are greatly appreciated," it adds.

Monument in cemetery

The cemetery is old. At one grave, a stone monument with a carving of a child in military uniform atop a horse, notes an 1844 birth, a 1907 death, and adds "gone, but not forgotten."

U.S. 450 passes a row of houses before it ends at U.S. 50 at the west edge of Shoals. Across U.S. 50 at the T intersection is an overlook onto the White River Valley far below. To the east toward Shoals is the Jug Rock, shaped, of course, like a jug. Shoals' most noted landmark, the rock is at least 45 feet high and 20 feet in diameter.

The county courthouse and Shoals' downtown district are over the hill near the White River bridge.

*   *   *

Ind. 450 is one of our favorite routes. It is usually free of traffic, the scenery is a diversion from most roads and each of the 25 miles is different.

INDIANA 446

FROM INDIANA 46 TO U.S. 50
Bridging Monroe

Ind. 446, one of Indiana's newest roads, is one of its most picturesque.

Built four decades ago to connect Ind. 46 and U.S. 50, it runs south from the east edge of Bloomington, crosses Lake Monroe,

eases around curves lined with trees, widens as it passes through sections of the Hoosier National Forest, then slices through chasms of limestone and enters farm land.

Routes lead off the road to the state recreation areas at the water's edges.

It is a 23.5-mile route designed more for pleasure than for speed.

*   *   *

Ind. 446 begins off Ind. 46, passing Bill Mallory (a former Indiana University football coach) Boulevard and other streets that lead west to housing developments.

A mile to the south it becomes an open road, the terrain changing from flat to hilly.

Curves are few until Ind. 446 reaches an area called Pine Grove where the Pentecostal Assembly meets in a log church.

Across the road is the Cabin (as in log) Restaurant and Lounge, where breakfast, lunch and dinner are served daily except Tuesdays. The Cabin is more than a place for food, karaoke bluegrass and country music and food. Firewood, stacked outside, is for sale as are beanie babies and other items inside.

Owner Janet Heston is at work at breakfast after working past closing time at 1 a.m. "It's hard to get good help," she explains, lamenting a frequent complaint from small business owners.

Another restaurant, the R & B Trading Post, is a short distance south. Around a curve is an obedience school for dogs.

Curves are continuous as the road angles slightly to the southeast as it follows Rush Ridge, where panoramic views open to Lake Monroe when the trees are free of leaves.

A regional headquarters for the Department of Natural Resources (with restrooms for those in need) is at the edge of Ind. 446 near a road to the Paynetown State Recreation Area.

As the road drops over a hill toward the lake it passes the gated entrance to the luxurious lakeside home of singer John Mellancamp.

Just to the south, the sun on clear days glistens on the water of Lake Monroe. Ind. 446 crosses the lake, which covers 10,750 acres, part of the 23,952 acres that includes six state recreation areas. One of those is the Cutright State Recreation Area off the south end of the bridge.

The road rises sharply from the lake, passes the Ransburg Boy Scout Reservation, then continues its twists and turns, passing the entrances to the Allen State Recreation Area and Hardin Ridge, a camp and picnic area.

This is a region where land was considered worthless before the Civilian Conservation Corps planted trees, the Hoosier National Forest bought some of the property, and Salt Creek was dammed to create Lake Monroe.

Just to the south is the Sixteen Corners General Store, which caters to those who fish and camp at the lake or ride the trails on horseback. It's a convenient stop for food, beer, wine, firewood, bait and fishing gear.

Ind. 446 is no longer narrow and winding. Shoulders are wide and paved. Turns are sweeping and gentle. Off to the southwest is Dutch Ridge Road, which is lined with small homes and a faint reminder of an oil well where crude was pumped for a short time around 1950.

Ind. 446 angles to the southeast as it descends around a curve, then cuts through limestone near the Monroe-Lawrence County border. To the east is Hunters Creek Road, which leads to another section of the Hoosier National Forest.

Ahead, the first farm fields visible since Bloomington are off the road in the bottom lands of Hunters and Henderson Creeks. Ducks swim in a pond near a Lawrence County road that leads west toward the Meadows Church.

The valley ends and Ind. 446 begins a 1.4-mile climb; the elevation rising from 573 feet to 700 feet above sea level through deep cuts in the limestone that forms a gorge.

It is not unusual to see rock hounds and geology students chipping chunks of the stone off the ledges in search of clues to the earth's creation.

Near the crest of the rise, a road leads west to the historic Gilgal Church and an adjoining cemetery, which dates back to 1830.

Ind. 446 declines from its peak and continues south, crossing Ind. 58 where signs point to Heltonville and a marker boasts the town is the home of Damon Bailey, an Indiana basketball legend. (See Ind. 58).

Homes sit on wooded lots on each side of Ind. 446 as it rises again, then declines slightly, passing the Mundell Church Road. Hereford cattle graze on a farm that has been in the Hunter family since about 1820.

Ahead is the Free Spirit RV Resort where campers and motor homes are parked amid hardwood trees that rise a hundred feet or more.

Ind. 446 ends a mile to the south at U.S. 50. The Farmers Market, a stop for deli food, snacks and gasoline is across the federal highway, which leads west to Bedford and east to Brownstown.

*   *   *

Ind. 446 is a pleasant road to drive in any season. It is more so in the spring when the redbud and dogwood bloom and in the fall when the sassafras is ablaze in red, and the hardwoods decorate the drive with color.

When caught behind towed boats or slow-moving vehicles, relax and enjoy the drive.

Columbus to Merom
In Search of a Destination

Call Ind. 58 a road in search of a destination. It twists and turns through small towns not much larger than the signs that identify them. Its direction varies, at times west, at times southwest, at times northwest, at times north. The longest straight route is less than ten miles.

On the map, it looks like a path laid out by a slithering snake on a cross-state journey.

The road connects I-65 south of Columbus with Merom 120 miles to the west, passing 22 villages and hamlets along the way.

Few other highways in the state are as divergent; their destination so uncertain. It is a road that provides the only links to other highways. It gives farms access to markets, rural residents a route to larger cities, travelers a view of a part of the state often overlooked.

And don't be surprised at some stop signs you'll encounter. Ind. 58 is one of the few highways that stop for traffic at intersecting rural roads.

*   *   *

Ind. 58 begins in the east at an interchange with I-65 five miles south of Columbus. An industrial park is on one corner, a huge convenience store at another.

A few small farms are amid rural homes as the road leads southwest to Ogilville.

OGILVILLE

Country Store

Ogilville is hard to pinpoint. It sort of drifts along the road, a series of homes on each side, with no other streets.

As we enter the community we recall a conversation a few years earlier with Irvin McCord, who lived his entire life in the area. He recalled that Ogilville was once called Sawmill, but had a post office with a "Moose's Vineyard" postmark. And it had a school, No. 4, "The only place I ever attended," he added.

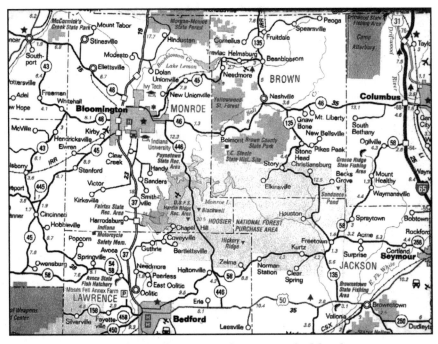

"The name Ogilville came later, probably because some Ogilvies used to live here," he said.

The school is gone and there is no post office. The community's centerpiece today is Meyer's Store, a popular stopping place for area residents and tourists and campers.

"Beer, wine, groceries, ice, lottery tickets, sandwiches, pizza, hardware, gasoline, bait, ammo," a sign at the store notes.

Meyer's is a father and son operation, Ed the father, Doug the son. It has the appearance of an old-time general store, but it now is more of a convenience stop with a country flavor.

On an earlier visit, Doug Meyer boasted that he makes the "world's finest" ham salad sandwiches from a secret recipe. "I've had people to tell me that, I'm not making it up. I've had people tell me that," he repeated. "Some strangers have said they've driven out here from as far away as Washington (D.C.) to taste my ham salad." He admits they may have been in the area, anyhow, but adds, "It makes me feel good, when they say that."

When in Ogilville try the ham salad or one of the other sandwiches. And while you are enjoying the taste take a look at the ceiling which has thin tin squares, coated with paint, that are a reminder of the past.

* * *

West of Meyer's store, Ind. 58 traffic stops at a three-way intersection with two county roads, then turns southwest and passes small farms, parallels a deep ravine and crosses a creek. An elementary school is in a community called Mount Healthy. To the south is the Mount Healthy Cemetery.

A sign at a small farm advertises "Fresh eggs, $1 a dozen."

WAYMANSVILLE

Problem Solvers

It's easy at times to get an education about life in small town Indiana. In Waymansville the place to do that is at mid-morning or mid-afternoon at the general store.

That's when retirees, farmers and other workers gather to sip coffee or soft drinks, swap stories and solve the problems of the world over coffee and conversation.

"We don't do breakfast any more, but we still have men who come in. We put in a second table to extend the "Liar's Club," explains owner Gretchen Bode, who bought the long-time store in 2000.

The small store advertises "live bait, beer and wine." It also is a deli and a place to buy groceries, ice cream and general merchandise. It keeps residents from having to drive out of town for a gallon of milk or a loaf of bread.

Besides, those men who gather here would have nowhere else to meet in the unincorporated village settled by families of German descent. St. Peter Lutheran Church remains as a part of that heritage. So does Lutheran Lake, a church camp with some permanent homes.

Youthful campers who are from cities, learn lessons in small town life when they visit the general store and listen to the stories spun by the men at the "lairs' table." So can adults who are generations from rural Indiana.

The road continues its zigzag course southwest from Spraytown through a tunnel formed by limbs that stretch out from trees on each side. Ind. 58 again stops for two county roads in Spraytown, then makes a 90-degree turn in the center of the tiny town.

SPRAYTOWN

Gathering Place

If Spraytown has a focal point it is Rucker's an emporium that is a combination grocery, hardware, restaurant and upholstery service with gas pumps out front.

Except for the Free Methodist Church, it's about the only gathering place in town. Chances are you will almost always find someone in the store engaged in conversation with owner Darrell Rucker or one of the clerks. On this trip, Rucker is away from the store. Two men, who appear to be loafers, are swapping stories.

A wall in the white concrete block building divides the grocery and restaurant business from the upholstery shop.

The Rucker's moved from Columbus several years ago to do upholstery and carpeting. "People wanted a store, so here we are," he told us on a previous visit.

Meantime he has grown to enjoy the daily repartee with customers. "We meet a lot of nice people," he said then. And we meet

some we wished the hell we hadn't met. You know how that is,"
he adds before a smile crosses his face.

Rucker's is a place to enjoy far from the impersonal Wal-Marts
or Meijer stores of the 21st Century.

*   *   *

Three miles ahead, around more curves and hills, Ind. 258
begins its route east to Seymour. Ind. 58 turns west toward
Freetown two miles ahead.

FREETOWN

Spartans Hangout

We remember Freetown from our youth. It was "the place" to
come each July 4 for an Independence Day celebration in the
wooded town park. Carnival rides and games of chance attracted
the young, political speeches and patriotic programs the old.

It was an annual event that continued into the 1990s when
carnivals sought bigger venues and visitors had other options.

The park remains in the unincorporated town. An elementary school remains nearby. Down the street is a metal covered
gymnasium, which looks more like a barn than a basketball palace. No matter. It was the home of the Spartans when Freetown
had a school. It still is in
use at times by youngsters
who seek to improve their
games and by adults who
seek to recover their youth.

If a visitor is fortunate
he may locate the township
trustee, or a designated
keeper of the key, for a look
inside. It will be deja vu for
those who remember when
every town had a school, a
basketball   team   and   a
sense of community.

Old Freetown Gym

High school students from the area now attend Brownstown Central.

Down the street from the gym, the Freetown General Store looks much as it has for 50 years. It is "home" each morning to "old fellers," as they are called. They've been known to arrive at 5:45 and spin stories until 10.

It is a full service store. Hardware is back behind the groceries. Out front firewood is for sale to campers who choose the Jackson-Brown County area for recreation.

A bank branch, a photography studio, a service station and a few other businesses also are in town.

*   *   *

Ind. 58 joins Ind. 135 at the west edge of Freetown and continues three miles south. Ind. 58 then turns west before curving its way past farms for four miles to Kurtz.

KURTZ

Old Cars and Memories

The town of Kurtz is off to the north of Ind. 58 along a fork of Salt Creek. A store on the highway is open at times, out of business at other times. A barber shop in a small building is closed. An Owen Township Volunteer fire station is nearby.

To the north, an old two-story building no longer is a general store. A Masonic Lodge remains. So does a Nazarene Church. Homes are scattered on the streets.

A Jackson County road leads northwest along the creek to the Hoosier National Forest and eventually the eastern edge of Lake Monroe.

Old cars and vans fill a yard and line the street at one home on a street that leads back to Ind. 58.

*   *   *

From Kurtz, Ind. 58 passes a cemetery then drops down a sharp decline into a valley between hills, crosses Tipton Creek and proceeds west. The lowland ends suddenly and the road twists around a steep incline, the elevation 876 feet compared to 609 feet two miles back to the east.

In Norman, Ind. 58 stops at an intersection with a county road, then makes a 90-degree turn through town.

NORMAN STATION
The Last Picture Show

Norman Station is a town where one man made a difference in the 1900s. It is a community where residents worked together in 2001 to save its restaurant.

First the man. He was C. E. Cummings an entrepreneur whose ingenuity helped keep the town alive during the Great Depression and for a decade beyond.

Among Cummings' enterprises was a general store, with gasoline pumps out front and furniture in the back. He also possessed a knack for salesmanship that would have made P.T. Barnum envious. Rural folks from miles around came to town each Saturday night when Cummings auctioned items from a platform at the side of the stores. As darkness fell he loaded reels into a projector and showed free movies on a building across the street, which by then was filled with viewers sitting on crossties and whatever seats they could find

The movies weren't very good, but the price was right and most of us (I was there every Saturday as a pre-teen) didn't know the difference, anyhow.

Youngsters with a dime could buy a three-dip ice cream cone, a bottle of pop or a bag of candy. They went home happy. So did their parents, especially those who thought they had found a bargain at the auction.

Two other stores were in town then. One closed, Cummings died and his business ceased several years later. The late Horace George kept the third store open into the early 1990s, but Norman was never the same. Cars allowed residents to shop elsewhere. Farms became larger, farmers fewer. Many families moved away to seek jobs elsewhere.

Today, there is no store in town, no gasoline pumps. There is a restaurant, thanks to the neighborliness of the people who remain.

It is where the residents of the 2000s come in. A little background: The Hitchin' Post, a restaurant where musicians performed on Friday and Saturday nights, closed when owner Jerry George suffered from brain cancer. Customers soon went to work to renovate and update the building, continuing their efforts after George died a short time later.

Within two months, the Hitchin' Post reopened with a new manager, a new menu and a new look. Men like sawmill owner Jerry Hall no longer had to drive seven miles to Larry Faubion's Heltonville Store for a sandwich. The women from nearby Kurtz again had a place to congregate. And the music played on on most weekends.

Stop in any morning and you'll find the locals—men and women—seated around a long table a few steps from the kitchen. If there is a world problem, they can solve it, or at least offer a proposed solution.

And it's good to know there are still small towns like Norman Station where residents think traffic gridlock is congestion on the streets of Seymour, population 18,000. "It takes forever to drive through that town on U.S. 50," one of the women complains.

Postscript: Over the years the name has been Norman at times, Norman Station at times. The signs at the edge of town now read Norman Station. The postal zip code book lists it as Norman.

*   *   *

In Norman Station, Ind. 58 makes two 90-degree turns, the first between the post office and the small frame church, then continues its route to the southwest.

In Zelma, another 90-degree turn directs traffic to the south.

Only a half-dozen homes remain in Zelma, which once was a stop on the Milwaukee Railroad. A canning factory is gone. So is a blacksmith shop, a store and a one-room school that doubled as a church.

A half-mile south of Zelma, Ind. 58 makes another 90-degree, this one to the west. The road runs straight for a time, drops down a hill, and continues four miles before stopping for Ind. 446. Ind. 446 goes north to Monroe Reservoir and Bloomington. Ind. 58 continues west into Heltonville.

HELTONVILLE
Community Pride

Ind. 58 does not run, it meanders, through Heltonville. It once crossed the now uprooted tracks of the Milwaukee Railroad three times between town limit signs.

Herman Ramsey describes the town best in this verse from a poem written in 1920:

> *"Sort of scattered in the valley*
> *And a-stragglin up the hill,*
> *Is a little Hoosier village*
> *By the name of Heltonville."*

Heltonville remains that kind of town although its general store, its feed mill, its barber shop and its restaurant are gone and its high school no longer exists.

The road now straggles up the hill past the Veterans Memorial, the Christian Church and the elementary school that once housed all 12 grades.

Near the crest of the hill, the road turns like an inverted V as it passes the school playground and a limestone tribute to Damon Bailey, who grew up near town. The road then continues down a slope where it passes the post office and the general store.

Both the Veterans Memorial and the marker for basketball legend Bailey reveal the character of the unincorporated town and its people.

The impressive Veterans Memorial was built by area veterans who raised the funds and did most of the work. It was a community effort not uncommon to the town, whose residents contributed funds to erect the stone tablet that lists Bailey's records at Bedford North Lawrence High School and at Indiana University.

Heltonville also is the home of the famous Turner Dolls. The factory, a mile north of town from the V in Ind. 58, makes vinyl and porcelain dolls for shipment around the world. The gift shop at the plant is open daily except Sundays.

Flags fly over Veterans Memorial at Heltonville

When in town, stop at Faubion's General Store. The ham salad and other sandwiches are good and someone will be there to answer any questions you may have.

As poet Ramsey penned:

> *"Your confidence is bolstered*
> *And your patriotism thrills*
> *When you think our mighty nation*
> *Is made up of Heltonvilles."*

*   *   *

Beyond the general store, the road makes a sweeping turn and begins a winding route west and south before making another 90-degree turn at a country crossroads. It continues to meander as it passes near Bedford North Lawrence High School and enters the north edge of Bedford. At times, the terrain is flat, more often rolling to hilly.

The roads enters Bedford as 5th Street and continues west to four-lane Ind. 37.

Just to the north on I Street is a branch of Oakland City College and a General Motors Company foundry. Off to the south is the heart of Bedford, "Stone City," as it is often called for the limestone industry that made it famous. Like most cities, its downtown is only a shell of its past, many of the businesses having moved out west near Ind. 37 and its shopping complexes.

Travelers can take one-way J Street downtown from Ind. 58 to the square and the 1930 Lawrence County Courthouse that is more functional than ornate. The County Historical Museum is in the basement of the courthouse that has a limestone exterior with extensive marble in the interior.

*   *   *

Ind. 58 turns north with Ind. 37 and follows the Salt Creek bottom as it skirts the west edge of Oolitic.

OOLITIC
Built of Stone

Oolitic, population 1,152, was built on the limestone that gave it its name. Dictionaries define Oolite as a small, round calcareous grain found in limestone. Oolitic is said to be a geological term for eggstone because the fossils in limestone resemble fish eggs.

A marker in Oolitic notes the nearby quarries have produced more building stone than any others in the world since 1850. If there is any doubt, the Indiana Limestone Company with a mill and acres of stone on its yards is at the main entrance off Ind. 37/Ind. 58 to Oolitic.

A ten-foot high limestone statue of Joe Palooka, the "world champion" boxer of comic strips of the mid-1900s, is on display in town. It was carved by George Hitchcock as part of the limestone industry's centennial in 1948.

Much of the town businesses is on old Ind. 37, now called Hoosier Avenue, which still links Oolitic and Bedford.

High school students now attend Bedford North Lawrence, but the Oolitic gym is open for basketball. A classroom in the old school is now a museum of local history. Oolitic Junior High and Dollens Elementary School are to the south on the old road.

Marian's Home Cooking, a popular eatery, is near the schools.

Oolitic is just two miles from Bedford but it has retained its identity as an incorporated town governed by a Town Council.

*   *   *

A short distance north of Oolitic Ind. 58 leaves Ind. 37 and joins Ind. 54 as it heads west through Avoca.

AVOCA

"Sweet Vale"

Oolitic's name comes from limestone. Avoca's identity stems from literature.

The name Avoca came, according to *Indiana: A New Historical Guide*, in an indirect way. Dr. Winthrop Foote, a Lawrence County pioneer who promoted the area's limestone for building uses, often retreated to a spring where he read Thomas Moore poetry that included a line:

> *"Sweet vale of Avoca,*
> *How calm I could rest*
> *In the bosom of thy shade*
> *With the friend I love best."*

The verse wasn't forgotten. Once a town was founded near the spring along Goose Creek, it was called Avoca. Avoca today is best known for the state fish hatchery to the south of Ind. 58/54.

A post office is on the highway as is the Avoca mini mart, "milk, gas. donuts and deli." Residences line the road as it curves through the community, a hill to the north, the creek to the south.

*   *   *

From Avoca, Ind. 58/Ind. 54 enters beef cattle country where rolling hills provide ideal grazing for livestock. Fields and pastures are fenced; homes are well-maintained en route to Springville. The Springville Feeder Auction lot at the east edge of town reflects the importance of cattle to the area's economy.

SPRINGVILLE
Gym Dandy

A restaurant ("homemade pies"), busy at breakfast, is on the highway at the south edge of Springville. So is a convenience store.

Anyone who fails to leave Ind. 58/Ind. 54, however, misses the real Springville. The town's landmarks are in the area to the north near Main Street and Popcorn Road.

On the main entrance to town are the Springville Grocery, two churches, the Springville Elementary School and the Perry Township Fire Department. An old general store, long abandoned, is in need of repair.

Old gymnasium at Springville

In good condition, however, is the Springville gymnasium. It has been six decades since Springville had a high school, but the home of the Hornets remains, a testimony to preservation. Built of native stone of various shapes held together by mortar, it is a reminder of the time when each small town had a school and a basketball team to bring it together on Friday nights.

A shelter house is adjacent to the gymnasium.

On the opposite side is the R & C blacksmith shop, a reminder of the days when muscled men forged steel, shaped horseshoes, sharpened plow points and made repairs farmers were unable to complete. Randy Phillips began the business in the late 1980s.

A week after our visit to Springville, Randy and Cammie Phillips, announced a sporting goods shop would be added to the location. "We are trying to branch out a little," Cammie Phillips told the *Bedford Times-Mail*, explaining that it was a down period for creating custom tools for the limestone industry.

*   *   *

A mile west of Springville, Ind. 54 exits from Ind. 58 and turns northwest. Ind. 58 swings to the southwest as it follows Spring Creek. A farm home in the valley is a reminder of architecture of the past, four vertical windows across each of its two floors. A door opens from the second level onto a veranda.

Beef cattle graze on the pasture beyond the house, the grass still green in early fall.

Lawrence County ends, Greene County begins as the road runs west along Town Creek toward Owensburg. Sycamore trees line the banks. A shop that sells and repairs golf clubs is on the north side of the road, a golf course just ahead, proof that golf is a popular pastime regardless of the location.

OWENSBURG

On The Rise

As are many southern Indiana towns, Owensburg is anchored on the side of a hill to the north above Ind. 58.

It is there on the slopes that an old store has been open, closed, reopened, closed and reopened over the years. It became Sue's Trading Post when Sue and Steve Owens reopened it in 2001, giving residents a place to congregate, sip coffee and buy whatever they need on the spur of the moment.

Nearby is the Emanuel Hatfield Museum Library, the post office, an antique store, now closed, and two churches.

It was Hatfield and Lilbern Owens who laid out the town in 1848 on the rise over Town Creek. And what an incline it is, the elevation rising from 626 feet in the valley 841 feet above Tunnel Hill to the north.

A tunnel that gave the hill its name was used by trains until it collapsed seven decades ago.

The Hatfield Library, part of the county library system, is a small frame structure open Saturdays and in late afternoons on week days.

Gone are most reminders of the businesses that made Owensburg a thriving town a century ago when dry goods, hardware and furniture stores were open, a flour mill operated, a hotel received guests and craftsmen made coffins at two locations.

Gone, too, is Owensburg High School, "home of the Indians," whose rivals included Solsberry. The two schools now are a part of Eastern Greene High.

Owensburg may be somewhat isolated in the southeastern corner of the county, but it is not beyond cyberspace. A web site for the Owensburg Baptist Church, which had its origins as a congregation in 1850, boasts it is a "warm and friendly" place to worship.

*   *   *

Just west of Owensburg, Ind. 58 is met by Ind. 45 which leads northeast to Bloomington. At the intersection is an entrance to the sprawling Naval Surface Weapons Center known as Crane. It is a high tech facility whose role is to acquire and maintain the Navy's weapons and electronic systems.

Ahead, Ind. 58 rises over what residents call Hard Scrabble Ridge, then runs straight before passing the Kentucky Ridge Church and scattered homes in what a road sign identifies as Doans. The town of Scotland is off the road to the south.

SCOTLAND

Tonsorial Treasure

Some advice to travelers. Do not fail to leave Ind. 58 and drive into Scotland. It's less than a mile into the town that is proud of its past.

A memorial in a small park atop the hill into Scotland is dedicated to Taylor Township veterans "who faithfully served their country in war and peace." Flags fly over the small but imposing setting presented to the town by the Scotland Historical Society in 1999.

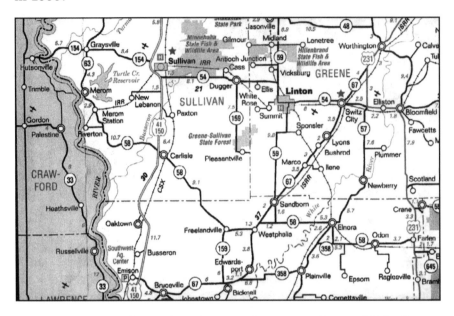

It is obvious the society is an active group. Down Main Street is the barbershop it bought, then renovated, as a reminder of the town's past. A barber pole remains in place on the tiny 12 by 18-foot building. Two liars' benches are out front.

There are no barbers in Scotland today. The hotel remains, the days when it accepted guests only memories. A general store no longer is open and the Toodie's, Too Café, is once again closed. Once a popular breakfast retreat for farmers and other workers, it has been closed, reopened, closed and reopened and closed again over the last decade.

One of the few businesses in town sells and services Snapper and other lawn and garden tools. On call is the Richland-Taylor Township Volunteer Fire Department which has a station in town near a shelterhouse.

A banner across Main Street promotes the Scotland Festival, held each year on the third Saturday in September. It features a parade with bands and floats, entertainment and crafts. And it gives visitors an opportunity to see the pride residents of small towns have in the past—and in the present.

*   *   *

A short distance from Scotland Ind. 58 joins southbound U.S. 231, an intersection with a convenience store called J. B. Junction. The road enter Daviess County, then continues toward Farlen. Off to the east on Ind. 558 is the village of Crane, which was built when the Naval base opened in World War II.

A farm market is at Farlen, a dot on the map. It is there Ind. 58 leaves U.S. 231 and turns west toward Odon, four miles ahead. The soil in northern Daviess County is rich and the crops are bountiful.

ODON

Open Door Town

Odon is a farm town that seems bigger than its population of 1,376. It has a town government, enough stores to make it a shopping destination, nice parks, an up-to-date library and a local newspaper.

It's small enough, though, to appreciate life far from mainstream America. It's a town where we observe a driver park, leave his pickup door open onto the narrow street and stroll into the post office, knowing other motorists would avoid a collision.

A half block away, two men seated on a bench in front of a store candidly share their thoughts about the town with a stranger.

"Nice town," one of them agrees, then laments the changing trends in merchandising as he looks across the street at the site of the old Odon Clothing Company. The locally-owned business, which once stretched almost a block, closed a few years ago.

A chain store, Dollar General, now occupies part of the building.

"Take Washington (the Daviess County seat)," he adds. "A Wal-Mart comes in and ruins its downtown and much of the whole county as far as small businesses are concerned."

Odon, though, still seems to have its share of home-owned stores. A furniture store, a pharmacy, a hardware, a gift store and a flower shop are near Spring and Main in the heart of the business area. Not far away are a lumber yard, a bank and a supermarket where Amish buggies are in the parking lot.

The Essen Haus, a popular restaurant, also is at Main and Spring. The decor is attractive. Waitresses are pleasant, greeting diners almost as soon as they are seated and filling coffee cups at breakfast without being asked. Owners Bob and Leann Wagler have made Amish cooking a specialty of the restaurant. If you are there for breakfast be sure to order the cinnamon rolls. And if you like grits, they are available, too, as is the "Sunrise Skillet," eggs, sausage, potatoes, cheese and gravy.

Food and shopping aside, Odon also is a place to relax. Concerts are held in the bandstand in the summer and walkers, joggers and bicyclists are welcome.

The park is the site of the annual Old Settlers Festival each August. The old-time celebration, said to be the oldest of its type in Indiana, features a parade, a carnival, local food delicacies, crafts and exhibits.

For visitors who wish to tour the area, Odon is the center of an Amish/Mennonite settlement. Drives over bucolic roads, many unpaved, offer views of men at work in fields with horse drawn equipment.

As a town, Odon is worth more than a casual visit. It's a return to a more pastoral era in American life.

                              *   *   *

Ind. 58 continues west from Odon, the farms along the route still productive. Off to the north is North Daviess High School, a union of Odon, Elnora, Epsom and Raglesville.

Five miles from Odon, Ind. 58 turns from west to north. Ind. 358 continues west to Ind. 57. Elnora is two miles ahead on Ind. 58 which offers a diversity of Daviess County's resources. Pumps bring crude oil from deep in the earth a few yards from huge turkey fattening houses.

Ind. 58 passes the Elnora Elementary School and enters Elnora as Odon Street.

ELNORA
Farmalls and Fordsons

A quiet town, usually, Elnora comes alive twice a year, once for the Daviess County Fair, once for the White River Valley Antique Association's show.

The fair in Elnora, population 721, is much like those held in other counties. The Antique Association's show, also on the fairgrounds, is unmatched, at least in Indiana. Acres of antique tractors, steam engines and other aged equipment are on display for three days each September. Craft, sales and food booths are numerous. Thousands of visitors come to town for a look back at farm life decades earlier.

Downtown Elnora appears to be only a shadow of its past. Many of the storefronts near Odon and Main are vacant. The post office, the Town Hall and the Long Branch Saloon are among the few places to congregate, except for Masons who have their own three-story hall.

Two convenience stores and a service station are in the town, once known as Owl Prairie and later Owl Town because of the great numbers of owls that inhabited the then wooded area. They were the genesis of the Owls, the sobriquet given to the Elnora High School basketball teams before consolidation closed the school.

Trains still run on the old Evansville and Indianapolis Railroad that allowed the town to flourish for a few decades before and after 1900.

*   *   *

Ind. 58 turns west again in Elnora, crosses the west fork of White River, which divides Daviess and Knox Counties. The J. Manfred Core Memorial Bridge spans the river as the road continues through the bottom land where the soybean and corn crops promise excellent yields.

(Core was state Democratic chairman when Matthew Welsh was governor from 1961 to 1965.).

Five miles beyond Elnora, Ind. 59 ends at Ind. 58 south of Sandborn, which was Core's home. A mile to the west Ind. 58 joins Ind. 67 and runs southwest for a mile toward Westphalia.

WESTPHALIA

A Class of Four

As southern Indiana towns go, Westphalia is young. Laid out in 1881, it was settled by immigrants some of whom came from Eastern Westphalia in Germany.

It grew up with the railroad to have a flour mill, a cheese factory or two, the usual blacksmith shops, a grain elevator, a general store and a hardware store, according to the accessknoxcounty.com web site.

A small restaurant, called the Country Charms Café in 2001, is on a triangle plot off the edge of the state highways. As have diners in other small towns, it has changed operators often over the years.

The Salem Cemetery and the impressive Salem United Church of Christ, which began as the Salem Evangelical Church, are on a slight rise. It was the church that sponsored a corporation that erected public housing units for rural senior citizens.

A cornerstone on the grounds notes the existence of the Westphalia School which graduated its first class of four seniors in 1914 and continued to operate until 1959.

A tavern remains open, but no longer serves the sandwiches for which it was noted. The grain elevator is closed and few other businesses remain.

Wesphalia is a farm community as quiet—and as peaceful—as the Vigo Township Public Library branch is when it is open a couple of days a week.

*   *   *

Beyond Westphalia, Ind. 58 turns as it passes a barnlot where three white horses gnaw on the damp grass. Ind. 58 again is a winding route as it passes a mountain of slag left from an abandoned strip mine. The terrain changes from flat to rolling.

There is little traffic. No cars back up behind a farmer on a tractor moving at 15 mph. The road turns south then west, the Bethel United Church of Christ on the corner. A spire that rises over the church and education hall is visible for miles.

Freelandville is a mile to the west.

FREELANDVILLE

Dutch Treat

It is obvious the German heritage remains in this town amid the rich farm land of northern Knox County.

"Willkomen - Freelandville - Established 1846," reads a sign at the east entrance to the town of 600 named for John Freeland.

In its 16 decades the town has seen elation and disappointment, but never hopelessness.

In the late 1980s, the *Farm Future* magazine called Freelandville "America's best little small town," noting it captured "the spirit of what made America great." It was a tribute that some residents still treasure.

Disappointment came when an era ended in the mid-1990s with the closing of Kixmiller's General Store, which had been a landmark since the town was founded. The upper windows are boarded, the store is empty, the doors are locked.

An "Oshkosh B'Gosh - World's Best Overalls! Kixmiller's" sign remains on the bricks of the two-story building. Like dozens of family operations, Kixmiller's, too, felt the competition of superstores that cater more to the dollar than to the community. An era, unlikely to return, has faded into history.

Kixmiller's was more than a store. It was a living history of a family and a town. John and Julie Ritterskamp opened the store in 1846. It continued to be operated by descendants until it closed.

Visitors to town can no longer visit the store and experience a journey back in time, a time 150 years ago when Freelandville was new and Kixmiller's was erected on town lot No. 1.

Across the street is the Dutchman Café, still without a sign after remodeling on this day in 2001. It is a story in itself. When a restaurant closed, farmers—known as the "Crop Crew" or the "Kraut Crew," depending on interpretation of the pronunciation—bought the building to insure it would continue to be operated. The crew still owns the building; two men own the restaurant and hire its operators.

To enjoy the camaraderie of farmers, plan to stop in the café during breakfast hours, then spend some time in the town that works to meet its own needs rather than expect help from elsewhere.

That's why a community organization built a 50-bed nursing home with a paid staff. It is how the Freelandville Housing Development, financed by the USDA, was started. And it is that pride that maintains Memorial Park where the bell remains from the old Widner Township School which closed in 1963.

Freelandville High School, home, fittingly, of "The Fighting Dutchmen," is now a part of consolidated North Knox. Stick around long enough and someone likely will mention the 1941 team that reached the Final 32 of the state basketball tournament.

It was another era of pride for "the best small farm town" in America."

*   *   *

Ind. 159 begins its six mile route south to Bicknell. Ind. 58 passes the Freelandville Christian Church as it leaves town, again changes directions as it heads twistingly toward Carlisle, ten miles to the northwest. An old farm home is accented by a second level veranda with a railing near where Knox County ends and Sullivan County begins.

The road makes another turn at Flowers of Christ Baptist Church and Bethlehem cemetery. Good farm land continues.

CARLISLE
Skirmish on the Wabash

Carlisle was a town before Indiana was a state, a pioneer county seat that notes a Revolutionary War skirmish fought on the Wabash River a few miles away.

James Ledgerwood is reported to have moved to the area in 1803, twelve years before his son, Samuel, platted Carlisle in 1815. The town was the seat of Sullivan County government for two years before it was moved to Merom and later to Sullivan.

A marker on what was to have been courthouse square notes the naval battle on the Wabash River, seven miles to the west, where George Rogers Clark's men captured seven British craft and 40 men.

Carlisle flourished when a railroad was built through town and thrived again when coal was discovered in the area.

That is the town's past. Its present is as a farm town surrounded by productive land, although a state prison out on U.S. 41 provides some employment. Census Bureau report showed the 2000 population had increased by 333 percent (from 613 to 2,660) when the prisoners were counted.

How many of those new "residents" are called "citizens" by the town is debatable.

The agriculture influence is obvious. The Growers Co-op is at the east edge of town off Ind. 58. Carlisle Farm Supply is off to the north.

A must stop in town is the Carlisle Hardware, a reminder of an earlier era. It is late summer and a sign advises: "Stock up on canning products—jars of all sizes." Out front on the sidewalk are wheelbarrows, shovels, rakes and assorted merchandise. Flyers cover part of the front, a town bulletin board of sorts.

There are few other businesses and some of the two-story buildings in the "downtown" area are vacant. The 1907 First National Bank is now the Sullivan People's Bank. A ladies' shop is open and a sign on a store front announces "Bright Beginnings" is coming soon. The Shatterbox appears to be the only diner in town except for a pizza outlet. An old filling station is now used for offices.

The Carlisle Elementary School remains in town. High school students, once known as Indians, now attend Sullivan High as "Golden Arrows."

Despite its long history, the name of the Ledgerwoods, who founded Carlisle, has not been forgotten. Ledgerwood remains as one of Carlisle's main streets.

*   *   *

Ind. 58 crosses four-lane U.S. 41 at the west edge of Carlisle and begins its 14-mile route northwest toward Merom. It is a road where one curve follows another, a route that appears to follow the slithering path of an inebriated snake.

An Odd Fellows cemetery is off the road. The soil, as dark as muck, has produced corn being harvested earlier than usual on this September day. At least one farm in the area has its own grain elevator. The last of the 2001 watermelon crop remains to be removed from a nearby field.

There is no traffic, except for an occasional truck, which is good because 90-degree turns are numerous as Ind. 58 winds through the rural area. Ahead a road leads to the west from a marker for Merom Station.

MEROM STATION
Unfulfilled Hopes

Some towns develop as expected, some do not. Merom Station never realized the high hopes that came when a railroad was routed through the area in the mid-1850s.

It never thrived like most towns along the tracks did when rails became the major mode of travel. The community today is a faint reminder of unfulfilled dreams.

The Merom Station Methodist Church built of concrete blocks sits amid trees. A grain elevator near the railroad is abandoned. Only a few homes remain on the two streets. One reflects the past, a restored steel-tired farm wagon on crushed stone surrounded by decorative brick on its huge lawn.

*   *   *

Ind. 58 continues toward Merom, passing the Perdue Farms turkey barns near an intersection of a road that leads east to New Lebanon. On the horizon ahead is the Merom Conference Center. Nearer town, an ecumenical sign for the Merom Conference Center and the United Methodist and Assembly of God churches invites visitors to "Come Visit With Us."

MEROM

Above the Wabash

Time seems to stand still here on this town high above the Wabash River. It is a good place to forget the time of day, or the day of the week, or the year on the calendar . . . at least for a while.

It is quiet and tranquil at Merom Bluff, the highest rise over the river of song and lore. We are alone in the park with our thoughts for no one else is here at noon on a weekday as we stand on a wall more than 150 feet above the river.

It is an opportunity to think of the town founders who named Merom for the elevated lake on the Jordan River, where in Biblical time Joshua fought a battle with kings.

A historical marker recalls the days of the annual Merom Bluff chautauquas that were held in the park from 1905-1935. They were ten-day religious and educational events—concerts, debates, plays and lectures designed to bring culture to the rural town. Carrie Nation, William Jennings Bryan, William Howard Taft, Warren Harding and Billy Sunday were among the speakers who came to town.

Entrance to Merom Center

It is quiet here in this scenic setting. We listen in the stillness and imagine those sermons Sunday preached, those speeches Bryan orated, the pleadings of Carrie Nation.

The town still has its Chautauqua Days, now annual three-day events the first weekend in June that bring hundreds of visitors to the giant shelterhouse, picnic grounds and benches.

Out across the vast bottom land of Illinois, giant grain elevators, silos and water towers rise from out of the horizon. Only the barks of a dog across the river, the lonesome caw of a crow in the valley break the stillness.

Merom, population 294, was founded as a town in 1817 and became the Sullivan County seat in 1819. Government affairs were conducted in a log courthouse until 1842 when a new courthouse opened in Sullivan.

A bell from the old Merom High School (now a part of Sullivan High) is in the small Town Park. Notices of meetings and hearings to be conducted by the Town Council are posted at the Town Hall. The post office is in the old Merom State Bank. Down the street are the Merom General Store and Café and McKinley's Coffee Café.

Except for Chautauqau Days, or quiet respites at the Bluff, the biggest attraction for visitors is the Merom Conference Center.

The center was once Union Christian College, which served as a preparatory school and college from 1859 until 1924. In 1936 it became Merom Institute, a rural enrichment center, and is now a camp, conference center and recreational area operated by the United Church of Christ.

No matter the reason for a visit, no one should leave Merom disappointed.

*   *   *

Indiana 58 ends at Merom. Its serpentine journey across southwestern Indiana is like life. Twists, turns, uncertainty, surprises, one moment, one mile, unlike any other. The road is seldom dull for each town is different and each experience a visual snapshot to be stored in the album of the mind.

It is a remarkable look at a part of the state and an insight into Hoosiers who live on a road less traveled.

INDIANA 63

Merom to Terre Haute
War and Peace

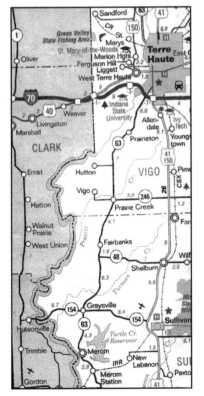

Ind. 63 starts in Merom, continues north through Terre Haute and extends to central Warren County where it ends at U.S. 41.

It is lightly traveled south of Terre Haute; a major four-lane traffic route to the north. It is 29 miles to Terre Haute, 89 miles to its terminus.

*　　*　　*

A few blocks from its origin in Merom, the road passes the Merom Cemetery. Part of the graveyard was the site of Fort Azatlan, said to have been erected by Middle Mississippian mound builders around 1200.

A historical marker at another cemetery (Johnson-Hopewell) a few miles north notes that Jane Todd

Crawford was the first woman to have an ovariotomy, a 25-minute surgery performed in 1808 without anesthetic by Dr. Ephraim McDowell in Danville, Ky. Mrs. Crawford recovered from the ordeal and came to live with a son in nearby Graysville, where she died at the age of 78.

In Graysville, Ind. 63 is crossed by Ind. 154, a link between Sullivan and Hutsonville, Ill.

GRAYSVILLE
Town Center

Ralph Ham is the essence of Graysville. Or Graysville may be the spirit of Ralph Ham. Whatever! He exemplifies the farm town, hard working, responsible, neighborly and unassuming.

Like the town, he now moves at a slower gait. He quit driving a school bus in 1995 after doing so for 40 years without ever missing a day. "Bought 10 new buses, one every four years," he told us on an earlier visit.

His achievement was a record that earned him a Sagamore of the Wabash award from then Gov. Evan Bayh and a tribute from the community that may have been even more rewarding.

Ham quit that job, but he didn't quit working. He still operates his Marathon Station, a place to buy gas, snacks, soda pop. It also is a story-telling emporium that, for men, may be the most popular spot in town.

A postmaster once told us, "Women congregate here, men go up to Ralph Ham's station."

We've stopped at the station a number of times over the last decade. It doesn't change, neither does the cast of characters. Nor does Ralph. He's been a friend since we first met. We—and the men who are here each day—are better for knowing him.

Not much goes on elsewhere in Graysville these days. Kids romp on the Graysville Elementary School grounds at recess; high school students having been sent to Sullivan High decades ago.

Graysville reflects the real Indiana. It's a place where folks care about each other and pretense is found only in a dictionary. A person's character is more important than his bank balance.

*   *   *

Ind. 63 crosses Turman Creek north of Graysville. We soon learn this is Turman Country. It is Turman Township and the old school at Fairbanks was known officially as Turman Township High School. The name is a tribute to William Turman, a pioneer farmer who worked the land long before many areas of the state were settled.

To the west is the Mann-Turman Prairie Center where graves are located on a prehistoric Indian mound. Not far from the cemetery is the site of Fort Turman, which was a communications link between William Henry Harrison's troops in Ohio and at Vincennes.

The land varies from woods to crop land as it approaches Fairbanks.

Ind. 48 begins at Ind. 63, just south of Fairbanks, on its 30-mile route southeast to Worthington. Ind. 63 continues into Fairbanks as Main Street.

FAIRBANKS
Neighborliness

It is quiet and peaceful as fall approaches. Fields of crops around Fairbanks are not ready for harvest. The post office and branch bank are open but there is little activity elsewhere.

A grocery closed a decade ago. So did a gasoline station/restaurant. Students who once attended Fairbanks High School as the Trojans, now attend consolidated North Central (Sullivan County) over on U.S. 41.

Times change, but residents have kept their small town values. "If you have a problem, there are people around to help," a woman tells us.

The area has not always been as serene. Its most notable event occurred long before Fairbanks became a town in 1840. A historical marker near town explains:

"A military action occurred in September during the War of 1812 three miles southwest of here. While escorting supplies from Fort Knox near Vincennes to Fort Harrison in Terre Haute, Sgt. Nathan Fairbanks and a dozen soldiers were ambushed." Most of the contingent was killed by Indians.

The town was named for Fairbanks (who some sources say was a lieutenant rather than a sergeant).

Fairbanks never grew much, having been bypassed by railroads. Residents may be fortunate it didn't. Bigger is not always better.

*   *   *

Sullivan County ends three miles north of Fairbanks and Vigo County begins. Farm fields continue to line the road as it approaches Prairie Creek.

Ind. 246 begins at Ind. 63 in Prairie Creek on its wandering route east to Vandalia near Spencer. Ind. 63 continues on toward Terre Haute.

PRAIRIE CREEK

Lost Identity

Once a town with its own identity, Prairie Creek today seems more like an adjunct to Terre Haute, 15 miles to the northeast.

High school students now attend Terre Haute South. No longer does a high school or athletic team give the community recognition or a sense of community.

A post office remains and the Jordan Junction convenience store on Ind. 63 is a place to stop for gasoline, groceries and snacks. The volunteer fire department and two churches are on the road through town.

*   *   *

A short distance to the north, Ind. 63 crosses Prairie Creek, the stream, which flows to the Wabash River.

The Hoosier Prairie Elementary School is to the north of town. Homes instead of farms are off the road as it heads toward Terre Haute.

PRAIRIETON

Blue and White

Just seven miles from Terre Haute, Prairieton has maintained its post office, an auto and truck service and a bakery, but it, too, is more a Terre Haute suburb than a rural town.

The volunteer fire department, in a deviation from the usual red, has a station painted blue, except for white trim. A department sign at the north exit from town tells visitors, "Thank you for coming."

*   *   *

Ind. 63 is also known as Prairieton Road as it heads northwest. En route it passes the Federal Prison, where bomber Timothy McVeigh met his doom, and the Graham Feed and Farm Center, an indication that agriculture remains a part of the area's economy.

The road enters Terre Haute from the southwest side. It joins U.S. 41. for a time, then leaves the federal highway and becomes a four-lane road near the Wabash River. It continues as a divided highway for 60 miles until it ends at U.S. 41.

South of Terre Haute it is a road less traveled. To the north it is part of a major route that ties western Indiana to the Chicago area.

INDIANA
236

Ind. 39 West TO U.S. 41
Small Towns, Big Fields

To reach Ind. 236, a motorist must first find U.S. 36 or U.S. 41, for this is a route that begins and ends away from a city or a town. It is a 40-mile route that illustrates a part of rural Indiana unchanged by urbanization.

In the east, Ind. 236 begins off Ind. 39 two miles north of U.S. 36 (at Danville), its immediate destination North Salem, eight miles to the northwest. It is not a route for speed. Curves are constant as the terrain rolls over rises that open to scenic vistas to the west.

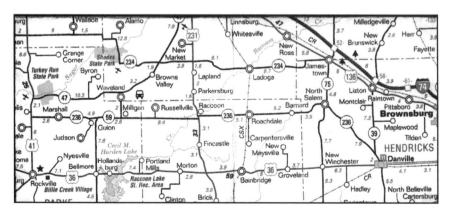

The drive is stimulating, not monotonous. Crests offer views spoiled only by man-made towers that speed communications at the expense of a horizon shaped by nature.

Old farm homes, courtly and historic, blend with newer houses minus the craftsmanship that defined the carpenters of a century earlier. An old cemetery is off to the east as Ind. 236 enters North Salem where it crosses Ind. 75.

NORTH SALEM
Old Fashioned Newness

North Salem is like gold. It's hard to find but worth the search. And more residents are finding it a place to call home, the population rising almost 100 to 591 in a decade before the 2000 census.

Businesses line a two-block section of Ind. 236, which is Pearl Street through town. Sidewalks inlaid with brick front restaurants, antique stores, craft shops and historic buildings.

An 1882 Independent Order of Oddfellows Building, an 1895 Masonic Lodge and an 1891 Town Hall are on the street. So is the United Methodist Church built in 1923, its stucco coating accenting its stain glass windows. The bulletin board advises readers, "Who you know will determine where you go."

North Salem Old Fashion Days Labor Day Weekend

The restaurants are the envy of residents of larger towns. Apple Annie's, with benches out front, promises "fine dining, steaks, chops and seafood" in an attractive atmosphere. The Red Dog Steakhouse and Saloon has been a popular destination for diners for years. And Liz's Country Café is a popular stop for workers and residents who want to start their days with coffee, breakfast and conversation among friends at a "liars' table."

Old Fashioned Days are an annual Labor Day weekend event in North Salem. It features antiques, entertainment, a car show, horse pulling contest, bed race, parade and other events.

It's a small town that has kept the enthusiasm of the people who founded it back in the 1830s.

*   *   *

Large, well-maintained homes are along Ind. 236 as it exits North Salem to the west. A mile or so ahead, a giant farm house remains from an earlier era. Hendricks County ends, Putnam County begins. The road crosses Big Walnut Creek near Barnard, a dot on the map with a few houses along the road, a cemetery and Mt. Olive Baptist Church.

Five miles ahead through farm land the road passes the Roachdale Cemetery and enters Roachdale.

ROACHDALE
Hardware and History

A "Welcome to Roachdale, established 1880" greets visitors to the Putnam County town. A grain elevator rises off to the north, reflecting the importance of the farm economy to the area.

Attractive older homes are along Ind. 236, the business area just to the north.

Most of the businesses are on Washington Street, among them a hair salon, a video games arcade, an auto repair shop, a building supplies outlet, a mini-mart , a laundry, a gift shop and Carey's Market where residents can buy "groceries, fresh meat and produce." The Roachdale Steakhouse Saloon is on the street.

None, however, match the history and the appeal (especially to senior citizens) of the Roachdale Hardware. "Stoves, implements, buggies and wagons, established in 1900," reads a sign on the side of the two-story business at 101 East Washington.

We weren't around in 1900, but chances are the store is a lot like it was then. A steel-tired wagon, a walking plow, the kind pulled by a team of horses, a hand cranked milk separator and other reminders of an earlier Indiana are on display.

This is not your box store Lowe's or Menards. This is your grandfather's hardware, the kind where you buy nails in bulk rather than in boxes and get personal service without running up and down aisles in search of a clerk.

That help usually comes from Charlie Riggle, the congenial owner for the last decade who knows the history of the century-old store. "The old place hasn't changed a whole lot," he says, showing pictures that date back to 1905. A 1913 photograph reflects a promotion for Majestic kitchen ranges in the days when wood stoves were used to make biscuits and pies and cook meals.

Among the photos is one of the 1935 Roachdale High School team that reached the Final 16 of the state basketball tournament.

Anyone who wants to walk back into the past can do so by stepping into the Roachdale Hardware from 7:30 a.m. to 5:30 p.m. Monday through Friday or 7:30 a.m. to 2 p.m. on Saturdays. That is except when the State Fair is underway. "I take a vacation then," explains Riggle, who deserves a hiatus after working 55 hours or so a week for 50 weeks a year.

The Roachdale Library is across Washington Street in a buff brick building.

Unlike many rural towns, Roachdale is growing, the 2,000 census showing a gain of 73 over the decade to 975. It's nice to know farm towns can survive. And even grow.

*   *   *

Ind. 236 continues to run due west through farm land from Roachdale. An old windmill is a remnant of an earlier time when it supplied water from a well to livestock.

The road stops at an intersection with U.S. 231, then runs south with the federal road for four-tenths of a mile before resuming its route to the west. The hamlet of Raccoon is just north of the intersection.

The Putnam County town of Russellville is five miles to the west on Ind. 236.

RUSSELLVILLE
Smile and Be Happy

Russellville may be only a ghost of a greater past, but pride among its citizens remains. A sign at Midland Co-op greets visitors at the east edge of town. Another welcome sign is in a garden-like setting on the south side of Ind. 236 where a county road leads a half-mile north into the community. Implanted among the flowers in the embankment is a "Have a Happy Day" greeting amid two floral smile buttons.

A quarry on the road into town is not in operation on this day. A Volunteer Fire Department is at the entrance to the town that grew up with the Baltimore & Ohio Railroad, then declined in population as the importance of rail transportation waned.

Russellville, however, did show a gain of four to 340 in the 2000 census.

In town, each side of a business block is lined with buildings whose roofs extend across the sidewalk. Except for the Town Hall, most of the storefronts are vacant and for sale. A corner market is closed.

Ron's 66 Service Station and garage is open at First and Harrison. It has the look of the 1940s when a motorist could drive into a roof-covered bay for gasoline and have an attendant check the oil and tire pressure and wash the windshield.

The Russellville Community Church is nearby, the Methodist Church down the street. A community park has a shelter house, slides and other playground equipment.

A grade school remains, but high school students now attend consolidated North Putnam. Memories of the town's 1921 "Bees" team that reached the Final Eight of the state basketball tournament are found only in faded newspaper clippings.

The post office is in one of the newer buildings in town. A bank remains open but there are few other businesses.

The Baltimore and Ohio depot remains, thanks to the foresight of those who saved it from demolition. Like the storefronts in town, it too is in need of renovation.

Pride in the town remains. It will take a community effort to return it to its more glorious past.

*   *   *

Back on Ind. 236, there is little traffic as the road deviates little from its direct route west. Putnam County ends, Parke County begins. Signs warn of horse drawn buggies, the choice of transportation for Amish who live in the area.

In Milligan, a wide spot in the road, a store is abandoned, but grain storage bins rise over the horizon. A woman walks across the road to her mailbox, the only evidence of life. We find no record for whom the town was named, but it may have been for John Milligan, one of the early landowners in the area.

To the west, Ind. 59 joins Ind. 236 for two miles before resuming its north-south route. Ind. 236 continues west, then arcs around the community of Guion, a one-time railroad settlement of a few houses. Rahn's Farm Market is the only business.

The terrain begins to rise and fall, indicative of Parke County's rolling terrain were streams are still spanned by 32 covered bridges.

After another sharp turn, the road again runs straight. Off the road a team of mules pulls a wagon of fresh vegetables from a truck farm where pickers continue to work.

The town of Marshall is four miles to the west.

MARSHALL

Signature Arch

Marshall may be just a gateway to Turkey Run State Park for some Hoosiers, but it's home to 360 residents.

It may be just a small farm town, but it has an attraction void in bigger places. An arch that spans Ind. 236 announces this is "Marshall" and gives the community its identity.

An arch on Ind. 236 is Marshall's signature

Two water towers rise over Marshall, which has a coffee and soda shop, a grain elevator and farms supply business, a printing company that offers silk screening and engraving, the Main Street Market, a bank and a few other businesses.

A Town Council oversees municipal government. High school students from the area attend Turkey Run High School as they have since 1958.

Ind. 236 makes a 90-degree turn to the north in the heart of town, then another 90-degree turn to the west. A county road leads north at the turn to Ind. 47 and the state park.

*   *   *

Ind. 236 resumes its bee-line west through farm land for three miles where it ends at U.S. 41.

It is a pleasant road to drive. There are few semis, few cars on most days. Each of the towns on the route has its own attractions. A visitor will not feel like a stranger wherever he or she may stop.

INDIANA
59

Waveland to Sandborn
A Drive to Enjoy

Ind. 59 mirrors Indiana's diversity as it passes through farm land and small towns. It skirts man-made lakes, covered bridges and strip mines before reaching its terminus in the rich bottom land of White River.

A motorist will encounter few big trucks or heavy traffic. It is a 71-mile drive to enjoy and to appreciate.

The road begins in the north off Ind. 47 at the town of Waveland, near Waveland Lake, or Lake Waveland, as it is sometimes called.

WAVELAND
Local Government

Waveland is an old town for west central Indiana. Pioneers settled in the area in 1822 and the first lots in town were sold in 1835. Businesses soon followed as did grist mills, a wagon factory and a hotel.

William Jennings Bryan, orator and presidential candidate, spoke in Waveland in the early 1900s when annual chautauquas featured lecturers, artists and entertainers.

The Waveland of the 21st Century is an incorporated town of 416 residents who are kept informed by an Internet web site with a number of links and the *Waveland Tattler*, "a positive news publication."

A Town Council manages local government, and an economic development committee works to attract economic growth. A park board oversees the park system, and town marshals patrol the streets and keep law and order.

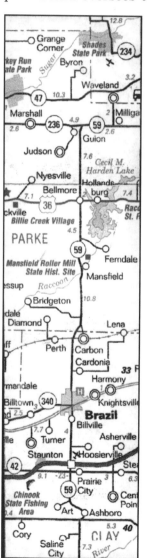

Ind. 59 enters Waveland as Cross Street, passing a grain elevator, a hardware and lumber outlet, a branch bank, flower shop, an antique shop or two, the Corner Market and Brenda's Kitchen, where residents can exchange the latest news over breakfast and dine at lunch and dinner.

Chances are a visitor won't be a stranger long if he mentions some Waveland High School basketball teams of the past. The Hornets, featuring stars like the four (Leonard, Ray, Keith and Bill) Greve brothers, won six sectionals before the school closed in 1971 and became part of Southmont.

American flags fly at many of the old homes as Ind. 59 leaves town. Brazil, the largest town on the route is 26 miles ahead.

*   *   *

South of Waveland, the terrain is gently rolling as the road makes a 90-degree turn. Montgomery County ends, Parke County begins. Two miles to the south, Ind. 59 joins Ind. 236 to the west for two miles before resuming its journey south.

The route through farm land undulates for a time, then flattens as the fields grow larger and the farms appear more prosperous.

Traffic on Ind. 59 stops before crossing U.S. 36 at Bellmore, an unincorporated crossroads community.

BELLMORE

Country Store

Bellmore isn't much more than a wide spot in the road, but it has kept the post office which gives it an identity . . . and stories about its past.

The post office, we were told, has been a fixture since the 1870s when the town's name changed from North Judson to Bellmore to avoid duplication of the North Judson in Starke County.

Legend claims John Moore, a resident at the time, had a daughter named Bell. He removed an "o" from his last name and came up with Bellmore.

The post office is in the Bellmore Country Store which offers general merchandise that includes groceries, meats, produce, hardware and automotive supplies. It also has bait and supplies for those who fish the lakes in the area. Gasoline pumps are out front where a box holds firewood for campers.

The store, circa 1930s, is said to have been built during the Great Depression by jobless men who laid the tile and did the carpentry work to help pay off the bills they had accumulated.

The Country Store isn't the only business in town. Across U.S. 36, the Big Berry sells sandwiches, ice cream and "the best cheeseburgers in Parke County."

A marine business is a stopping point for those who visit Raccoon Lake, which is just a long cast away.

*   *   *

Ind. 59 continues south. A ramp to Raccoon Lake is off the road. The first curve in miles comes south of Bellmore. Farms end for a time and woodlands line the road as it nears Mansfield, a village east of the highway.

MANSFIELD

Tourism Is Its Business

It's best not to visit Mansfield during the Parke County Covered Bridge Festival if you wish to enjoy the hamlet's scenery and the history. You may be overwhelmed by the crowds and the hundreds of crafts stands that occupy the grounds.

It is a more serene, peaceful place at other times and the antique shops can be visited at leisure from April through October.

If, however, you like crowds, Mansfield, in addition to the Covered Bridge Festival, is host to the Mushroom Festival in April, a Bluegrass Festival in June, a Gospel Sing in July and an Old Fashioned Christmas in December.

Mansfield's covered bridge

The major attraction for history buffs, however, is the Mansfield Roller Mill, now a state historic site. The wooden frame mill, built on the banks of Big Raccoon Creek in 1875, rises three stories above the valley from a sandstone foundation. Most of the turbine-powered equipment remains in place.

Wheat was ground into flour at the mill for decades. The power from the mill also was used at times to saw lumber and to card wool. Times changed, water power became less important, and by the mid-1900s the building had become a feed mill. A state historic site since 1994, it underwent renovation in 2001.

Another attraction is the 247 feet long, double span Mansfield covered bridge over the Big Raccoon. It was erected by Joseph J. Daniels in 1867.

The Mansfield Bible Church looks to be almost as old as the town. Out front a statue of a boy holds a fishing pole and a sign that reads, "Come and I will make you fishers of men."

*   *   *

Ind. 59 continues south from Mansfield. A rural road leads five miles west to Bridgeton, another Parke County town with its own covered bridge. Parke County ends, Clay County begins south of the road to Bridgeton.

CARBON

Sawing Logs

Carbon, population 334, is east of Ind. 59, past the sprawling Pike Lumber Company mill, past the water tower and across the Conrail tracks where trains drown out the noise of timber being sawed.

A Town Council oversees municipal affairs. The three-story brick Independent Order of Odd Fellows Building with a cornice across the top appears to be the biggest building in town.

Businesses are few, making the post office and the Town Hall the centers of activity. A Clay County Park is in town, but the shelterhouse and playground are vacant at mid-day.

Three churches, Methodist, Baptist and Nazarene, are in the area.

If Paul's Place remains, it no longer is identified by an exterior sign. We recall a previous visit at mid-morning when men sipped beer and solved the problems of the world.

Like elsewhere, nothing is forever in Carbon.

*   *   *

Two miles south, Cardonia is another unmarked hamlet east of Ind. 59 at an intersection of Rio Grande and another Clay

County road. "Carbon has a marker to it on Ind. 59. I don't know why there can't be one for Cardonia," a resident complained.

A store that once kept residents of the community from driving to Brazil for a loaf of bread or a quart of milk no longer is open.

Brazil is two miles to the south, past a rose garden, homes and businesses.

BRAZIL

National Road

Ind. 59, lined with well-kept homes and businesses, enters Brazil as Forest Avenue.

In the heart of town, Ind. 59 crosses U.S. 40, the old National Road, which is Brazil's main thoroughfare. An ever-present CVS drugstore is at one corner. The old post office near the intersection is now a museum.

The city, named for the South American country, grew up with the National Road and prospered when trains began to run through town. It now is a city of 8,188 residents in the eastern shadows of Terre Haute.

U.S. 40 remains Brazil's main business and shopping avenue, although much of the transient traffic has been diverted out to the south on I-70.

Old stores, most of which are occupied, are on U.S. 40. To the east is the Clay County Courthouse, the seat of government since it was moved from Bowling Green in 1877. (See Ind. 46).

From U.S. 40, Ind. 59 passes Forest Park a short distance to the south. The park has two restored log cabins, a pool, and shell, tennis courts and a golf course.

*   *   *

Ind. 59 runs under I-70 four miles south of Brazil, intersects with Ind. 46 and continues its route south.

The village of Ashboro is off to the east. It is another town that lost its identity when its school closed and its students, known as the Shamrocks, were sent down Ind. 59 to Clay City. About all that's left in town are a few houses and a gun shop.

A four-way stop is to the south where Ind. 59 crosses Ind. 46. A restaurant and convenience store are at the southwest corner.

Land, a mile to the south, has been uprooted and a pit opened for a strip mine, this being coal country. A county road leads past the site west to Saline City.

SALINE CITY

Memory Lane

Saline City is another town that is a specter of its past. Its old general store is closed, a Camel cigarette advertisement the only sign on the two-story building with a roof across the front.

Gone, too, are the dry good stores, a stave factory and a hotel that operated when the small town thrived and residents did not have to drive to nearby cities to shop.

A pump, its handle in place, is a clue to the days before homes had indoor plumbing.

Thirty, maybe more, homes are in town, but there are no stores, no post office, no businesses. A Clay County park at the east edge of town is the scene of an annual Labor Day reunion when residents gather to recall the days when coal was king and Saline City was a busier town.

*   *   *

South of the road to Saline City, a historical marker on Ind. 59 near Eel River notes the site of the Crosscut Canal. The waterway connected the Wabash (near Terre Haute) and White River at Worthington. Work on the connection started in 1836, was abandoned in 1839, then resumed to be completed in 1850 as part of the Wabash & Erie Canal.

A short distance south, Ind. 59 enters Clay City as Main Street.

CLAY CITY
Midwest Mayberry

Snobbish visitors may scoff at Clay City's designation as "The Mayberry of the Midwest." That's their loss. Such haughtiness could keep them from enjoying the informality of life in small town Indiana.

It's hard to dislike a town that has pride in its own worth and the confidence to withstand occasional taunts.

You won't find Sheriff Andy Taylor or deputy Barney Fife here. You will find residents with the down-home easiness that made the fictional Mayberry and its lovable citizens a long-running television show void of pretense.

As in fictional Mayberry, pomposity is an alien word in Clay City. It's a town where we once saw a resident bring her own jar of jelly into a restaurant to spread on the toast she ordered.

Clay City, to some visitors, is "a town in a time capsule." To others it is "a throwback to the days when people waved to friends, knew neighbors on a first name basis and took time to enjoy visitors."

In reality Clay City isn't a city at all. It's a town of 1,019 run by a Town Council, and promoted by citizens who want to share its virtues with others.

The town has more than 50 businesses that include a newspaper, two banks, two car dealerships, a medical center, a supermarket, a pharmacy and restaurants. It also has been home to the Clay City Pottery Company since 1885.

A Pottery Festival in June is an annual event as is the Clay City Fair in July.

Clay City has kept its high school, adding students from Ashboro, Cory and Bowling Green in a consolidation. The school athletic team, the Eels, have done well in basketball and baseball, and the band has won at least five state division championships and performed at one presidential inauguration in Washington.

Clay City, its residents say, is "Hoosier Hospitality, the friendliest town in Indiana." Anyone who comes as a stranger and leaves as a friend, will find that the case.

*   *   *

In Clay City, Ind. 59 joins Ind. 246 for two miles where it resumes its route south at the village of Martz.

Wooded areas are along the road before the terrain opens and fields reappear. Open spaces continue for seven miles until the road again crosses Eel River.

A second marker notes another part of the Crosscut Canal, 1850-1861. Land sales in Clay County, it explains, helped finance part of America's longest canal, the Wabash and Erie, which extended from Lake Erie to Evansville.

Near the river, Ind. 59 makes a turn to the west into the village of Howesville. Only a few houses and a small frame Presbyterian Church are in the town surrounded by farms.

Ind. 59 stops at a T-intersection two miles to the south before it makes a 90-degree turn south. It is obvious we are in Bogle Corner. An American flag flies over a "Bogle Corner - USA" sign. Another sign at a rock garden greets motorists with "Hi! Bogle Corner." A few houses are in the hamlet where residents take pride in playing a small role in the life of the nation. A short distance to the south Ind. 59 crosses Ind. 48 at the east edge of Jasonville. Ind. 48 goes west into the heart of town.

JASONVILLE

"Best Little Town"

Jasonville calls itself the "Gateway to Shakamak," but it's more than that. It's a city of 2,490 (up 13 percent from 1990) residents governed by a mayor and city council.

It also is a business center of northwestern Greene County where residents can shop for food, buy furniture, stop at the town library, subscribe to the *Jasonville Leader* and dine at restaurants.

It also is home to Shakamak High School, a consolidation of Jasonville, Coalmont and Midland.

Few old buildings remain, major fires in 1914 and 1967 having devastated the business area.

Once a coal mining town, it is now a resort community where visitors meet en route west to Shakamak State Park, its campgrounds, three lakes and aquatic center.

Jasonville advises visitors it has "the best of everything" with a "small town friendly atmosphere . . . local businesses, parks, churches and services." It is, it asserts, the "Best Little Town in Indiana."

One place to appreciate that small town atmosphere is at Sharon's Kountry Kitchen. The decor alone is worth a visit to the corner two-story brick. The tables are covered, the paneled walls are decorated with plaques, posters and dozens of pictures of the Jasonville of an earlier time when coal was the city's main industry.

Colorful menus offer extensive selections for breakfast, lunch or dinner. We have found the food excellent whatever the meal, but the barbecued baby back ribs are unmatched.

Anyone who stops at the Kountry Kitchen is likely to meet owners Sharon and Bill Boyd and enjoy conversations with farmers, coal miners, families and business leaders who make it their restaurant of choice.

*   *   *

Ind. 59 continues south from Ind. 48 at Jasonville. It is three miles to Midland.

MIDLAND
"Beat The Rush"

Midland may have lost its school and what businesses were in town, but it hasn't lost its sense of humor.

A sign at the Midland Baptist church, established in 1856, advises residents on this warm late summer day:

"Beat the Christmas Rush. Come This Sunday."

This is another town that thrived when coal was king, then languished when the demand lessened and cars allowed residents to drive to larger towns to shop.

The residential community of modest homes is on the west side of Ind. 59. The church and a park are on the east side of the road. A bell from the old Midland High School is in the park as is the school's alumni shelterhouse. A ball diamond, no longer in use, is now a grassy field.

Students from Midland now attend Shakamak High where its athletes are known as Lakers.

*   *   *

Ind. 59 continues due south for five miles where it joins Ind. 54 three miles northwest of downtown Linton. Businesses and restaurants are along the route into the Greene County city.

Ind. 54 continues through Linton as A Street. Ind. 59 leaves Ind. 54 at Main Street where it resumes its route to the south.

LINTON
"You'll Like It"

Anyone who thinks Linton is just another small Indiana city is wrong. It surpasses expectations for most visitors.

Wrought iron arches stretch over entrances to the city promising visitors, "You'll Like Linton." It was selected as the city's motto in a contest 75 years ago and remains its signature today.

A population of 5,774 makes Linton the largest community in Greene County even though the county seat is at Bloomfield. A mayor and city council oversee the city in the heart of coal

One of arches at main routes into Linton

country where Linton High School athletic teams are known as the "Miners."

The annual Freedom Festival includes an Independence Day parade, a carnival, an arts and crafts show, musical entertainment, fireworks, motorcycle races, a horse pulling contest, and a gospel sing.

Another big event is the annual Phil Harris Celebrity Weekend in honor of the town native who became a noted entertainer. The event features a golf tournament at the Phil Harris golf course where Harris played until his death in 1995.

In the business area on Main Street, some buildings are vacant and for sale. Other stores occupy the street levels of buildings a century old. A variety store that has survived the arrival of discount stores is in the Wolford Block. Diana's Paint and Wallpaper Company is in a two-story corner building decorated in attractive green tones.

The library is in a 1892 two-story-brick still well-maintained. The City Hall, dated 1912, appears to be much newer than that.

Among 17 restaurants are Stoll's Country Inn, the Happy Greek Café, Old Bank & Company, The Grill and the usual fast food restaurants.

Probably the best known diner is The Grill, owned by Jim Cary. It may not serve the biggest meals or have the best atmosphere but it is a Linton landmark known by customers throughout the area since 1922.

A "United Mine Workers" sign is on a clock, but that doesn't keep management, lawyers, doctors, store owners, farmers and tourists from feeling at ease at The Grill.

Stop in Linton. You'll like it. Would a sign that has said so since 1926 lie?

*   *   *

Ind. 59 continues south from Linton over rolling terrain and past farm fields. Buildings where turkeys once were fed are empty. The fields around them are fallow.

Greene County ends, Knox County begins. Sandborn is across Ind. 67 to the south. A smaller service station is closed, a victim perhaps of a larger mini mart on the northwest corner of the intersection.

SANDBORN

Peace and Quiet

Sandborn was platted in 1868 as a stop on the Indianapolis and Vincennes Railroad and named for a surveyor who helped chart its route. By 1900, it had become a bustling town with a cheese factory, a hardware, general stores, meat markets, a five-and-dime, a hat shop, a hotel and restaurants.

No longer a railroad station, it now is a four-way stop on Ind. 67 between Indianapolis and Vincennes where motorists can stop for fuel and snacks at the convenience store.

Its best-known citizen may be John Gregg, speaker of the Indiana House, who hosts a talk show each Saturday on an Indianapolis radio station. Anyone who hasn't heard of Sandborn hasn't tuned in to his program.

Ind. 59 runs north-south though the farm town of 450 residents as Anderson Street, passing the Town Hall, Fire Department, Lions Club Building, a branch bank and a chapel in an attractive building with four columns across the front. A big agricultural service center is along Ind. 67 for this is a town near the rich bottoms of the east fork of White River.

A baseball diamond is in a small park on the east side of Sandborn, whose governmental affairs are managed by a Town Council.

High school athletes from town who once were the Sandborn Blue Jays are now the Warriors of North Knox, a consolidation of Sandborn, Bicknell, Bruceville, Edwardsport, Freelandville, Oaktown and Westphalia.

Not much happens in Sandborn these days, except an occasional outing in the park. It's a quiet place far removed from the noise of a city or a traffic gridlock. Most cities and towns should be so fortunate.

*   *   *

Ind. 59 ends a mile south of Sandborn at Ind. 58. The drive has made us appreciate the people and places along the route.

INDIANA 42

Mooresville West to Terre Haute

Across West Central Indiana

Ind. 42 begins inauspiciously at an intersection with Ind. 67 at the southeast edge of Mooresville. Its destination to Terre Haute 65 miles to the west is unmarked. The road passes through farm lands, small towns and depleted coal fields as it stretches across west central Indiana.

MOORESVILLE

The New and the Old

Call this a countrified city or a cityfied country town. It is, at the start of a new century, difficult to tell which it is.

The pioneer town Samuel Moore founded in 1823 between the east and west forks of White Lick Creek has mushroomed into a suburban Boomburg. Its roots are country, its future appears headed for urbanization.

A quiet town a half century ago, it grew when Ind. 67 was widened to four lane, a bypass skirting the edge of town. It soon became a commuter community for wage earners who choose to live in town and drive to work in Indianapolis.

Restaurants, store and businesses followed in time. Franchises replaced entrepreneurship. Houses and box stores grew on

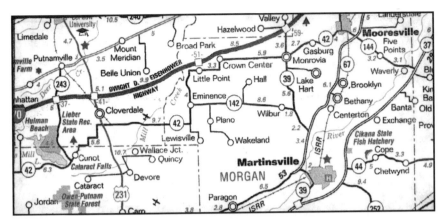

land that once raised corn, soybeans and wheat. Development, clustered around Ind. 67 exits, has been more slipshod than orderly. The result the same unsightliness as that found in a dozen other communities on the fringe of Indianapolis. Quality of life suffered in the pursuit of property tax revenue.

By Year 2,000, the population had reached 9,273, an increase of 67.4 percent over the 1990 census.

That's the citified view of Mooresville. A countrified look remains in the heart of the older section of town where historic buildings still stand and most residents live on quiet tree-lined streets.

Merchants in the business district are seeking a historic designation for the downtown area as part of its continued revitalization.

And this is a town with history. It was here the Friends Church held its first meeting in 1823, and it is here they still gather in an 1884 meetinghouse. A block to the north is the Friends Academy, operated by the Quakers from 1861 until 1870 when it was bought for use as the Mooresville school. The remodeled academy is now home to the Mooresville Historical Society and the Morgan County Community Foundation.

Both are on the campus of Newby Elementary School, once the town's high school. On the grounds is a remodeled 70-year-old-gymnasium built—and restored seven decades later—with community support.

When in Mooresville tolerate the development on Ind. 67. Enjoy the old part of town. It is worth seeing.

*   *   *

Ind. 42 eases west through Mooresville on High Street, where old homes once made it silk stocking row, crosses the west fork of White Lick Creek and begins a rolling, curving route toward Monrovia.

*   *   *

"York Farm," notes a sign on a barn on one of the curves. It is a prime site for development and the farm, its rolling acres and its location coveted for home sites by developers. Gregory Orchard, a family fixture for 75 years, is a short distance to the west.

The Midway Auction School is in an old general store in tiny Gasburg, a hamlet midway between Mooresville and Monrovia. Ahead to the south of Ind. 42 is Greendell Farm, which has combined mulch sales with plant sales to create a growing business.

Another of Morgan County's pioneer Friends meetinghouses is on Ind. 42 as the road approaches Monrovia. Like the one in Mooresville, West Union was organized in the 1820s, built a church in the 1830s and later started a school.

MONROVIA
Changing Times

Monrovia, one of Indiana's newest towns, is in transition. It is moving from a farm-centered village into a suburban town, its newer residents as interested in business trends outside the area as they are in crop yields on the fertile fields that surround them.

Growth caused the town to give up its unincorporated status in the mid-1990s when a Town Council was elected to manage local government. A marshal now patrols the streets instead of an occasional Morgan County deputy.

Change has not been easy. Some residents, unaccustomed to restrictions, have been critical of home rule and regulations. Others resented uprooted streets and problems caused by installation of a new sanitary sewer system for the 628 residents.

And more growth, bringing additional changes, is expected. Ind. 39, which intersects with Ind. 42 in Monrovia, is but three miles south of I-70, an easy route to jobs in Indianapolis. A farm at the west has been sold at auction, its development for homes and businesses almost certain.

Unlike other small towns, Monrovia kept its high school despite consolidation. Enrollment has stayed on an upward trend to around 450. The school's Bulldog basketball and football teams have had continued success in tournament competition, players winning athletic scholarships to colleges.

Change is evident in the two-block long business district downtown. A new Subway/ice cream shop opened in early 2000. Zydeco's, featuring authentic Cajun, Creole and New Orleans cuisine, has been a success. Other new businesses have opened.

The transformation from rural to urban will continue. The secret for those who direct Monrovia will be to balance growth with quality of life.

*   *   *

From Monrovia, the road runs due west six miles through some of Indiana's best farm land to Crown Center, which isn't much bigger than a curve around a Christian Church. A short distance to the south, the road makes another 90-degree turn.

Little Point, a dot on the map near an I-70 interchange, has a convenience store and a trucking company. A garage and wrecker service is on call frequently as it responds to the inevitable accidents that occur on I-70 as well as narrow county roads.

Beyond Little Point, Ind. 42 turns south and makes four sharp turns as it heads toward Eminence. The road is lined with soybean and corn fields where crops have flourished in the warm, wet summer of 2001.

Two plantation type homes are amid those more modest.

EMINENCE
Bucking Trends

Its isolation may be an asset for Eminence. It's too far from I-70 to attract many commuters to jobs in Indianapolis and developers are not yet turning nearby farms into home sites.

Eminence remains rural, mostly unchanged over the decades. Oh, there may be a few new businesses like the hardware store, but folks still shop at a store called the Trading Post, buy gasoline at the Marathon pumps, bank at a branch of a Mooresville bank, dine at a small town café, pick up the mail and maybe a bit of gossip at the post office. If its too far to drive to a movie, they buy a film at the video outlet and watch it at home. And everyone knows—and cares—about most everyone else.

And people here are a bit independent, too. They defied the trend to consolidation and kept the high school despite an enrollment of only 150 in the top four grades.

Fans of Eminence athletic teams still recall the 1962 Eels basketball team that reached the Final 16 of the state tournament and the 1978 squad that won the school's second sectional.

Eminence remains unincorporated, its only government in the hands of the county commissioners and other office holders at the Morgan County Courthouse in Martinsville.

Residents here are yet to be convinced bigger is better.

*   *   *

South of Eminence, Ind. 42 makes a right turn to the west at a four-lane stop. It is suggested that those who appreciate nostalgia continue south for a mile to Lewisville, a crossroads of a few houses and a general store that remains from an earlier time. A roof covers the porch of the two-story masonry building entered through double screen doors. Inside hardwood floors are laid diagonally. The high ceiling also is tongue-in-groove wood, a reminder of a time before plasterboard became a builder's shortcut.

The store doesn't pretend to be a Wal-Mart or a Kmart. It is, however, a place for area residents to buy items, share time with neighbors and enjoy a way of life before it vanishes from rural America.

Back on Ind. 42, the terrain no longer is flat. Morgan County ends, Putnam County begins. A short distance ahead, the road crosses Mill Creek.

Ind. 42 meets U.S. 231 at the south edge of Cloverdale

CLOVERDALE

In The Clover

Cloverdale's business district is not the same as it was a decade or more ago. It's better, neater. Signs of revival have followed the widening and improvement of U.S. 231. New buildings have opened, others have been improved.

Credit part of the change to Main Street, an organization that seeks to improve the quality of life and revitalize old downtowns. Credit part of the change to local merchants who have chosen to stay put and help with renewal rather than relocating to the edge of town and add to the unattractive sprawl out toward I-70. Thank the town's 2,242 residents who continue to shop with local merchants.

Motorists who exit I-70 for gasoline or food do not see the real Cloverdale. What they notice is the usual clutter of motels and fast food franchises. The heart of town is a mile to the south. It is there the local entrepreneurs are located; it is there residents are almost oblivious to the rush of life out to the north.

Like Eminence, Cloverdale has kept its high school, despite an enrollment that seldom exceeds 425, and its sense of community. Chances are a visitor won't be here long before a basketball fan recalls the success of the Cloverdale Clovers' basketball teams from 1965 to 1983. Coach Jim Miller's team went to the semistate in 1965, then made it to the state finals a year later. Al Tucker coached seven sectional winners from 1968 to 1983, the year the Clovers were among the final 16 teams. It was a time before class basketball, when the Cloverdales of the state competed for championships with schools ten times larger.

*   *   *

Ind. 42 makes a number of sharp turns as it heads southwest from U.S. 231 at Cloverdale. A golf course is off the road, so are three churches within a mile of each other. A farm home with a white picket fence is at the corner of a 90-degree turn. Putnam County ends, Owen County begins.

The Ten Commandments are posted at a junk yard lined with rusting cars.

Near Cunot, a community with undefined limits, Ind. 243 leads north to the 8,075-acre Lieber State Recreation Area. The park has campsites, a beach and wooded areas. To the west is the 1,400-acre Cagle Mills Lake, formed by a 148-foot high dam across Mill Creek.

It is possible to reach Cataract Falls, another area attraction, by car, but it is best to ask a local resident for directions. Beyond the falls is the village of Cataract, where the Cataract General Store is a must stop for anyone interested in a look back in time.

Cunot is a mixture of homes, bait shops, restaurants, small food stores and an outreach mission. A community center and a senior activity building, with "bingo on Tuesday nights," also is on Ind. 42 as it winds its way west through an area more suited to recreation than farming. Owen County ends and Clay County begins a short distance east of Poland.

POLAND

Historic Site

Don't drive through Poland without stopping. There's always someone to talk with in the hamlet tucked away in an eastern pocket of Clay County.

A visitor soon gets the idea it's a friendly town. "Poland - Established 1841 - Welcomes You," greets a sign amid a triangular flower bed accented with small American flags.

The Poland Hardware, "sales and service, bait and tackle," reports it is under new management, Jimmy Spelbring by name.

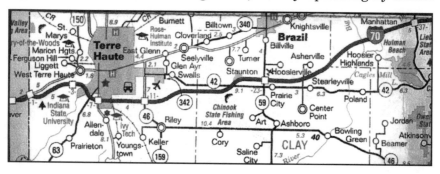

The store is in an old two-story frame building that appears to have weathered much of Poland's life as a town.

A post office and bank are a few steps away.

Across Ind. 42 is the Hillman Market, "your complete country store—milk, eggs, bread, butter, and gasoline." It's not only a store, it's a place to sip coffee, relax and catch up on what's happening around the unincorporated hamlet.

It also is a picture gallery with some excellent photos taken by owner Jerry Hillman on display. His pictures include scenes—barns and natural attractions—from around the nation, among them a memorable picture of a lighthouse on Lake Superior.

Hillman, who left his job with the advertising department of Indianapolis Newspapers in the late 1980s, still enjoys the tranquillity of the area. Being your own boss has its rewards.

Poland Historic Chapel

Two blocks or so to the west is the Poland Historic Chapel, a white clapboard covered frame building with a bell in the tower. Both the church and the cemetery are on the National Register of Historic Places. The Gothic-Revival-style chapel was dedicated in 1869, three years after a Presbyterian church was organized.

*   *   *

Ind. 42 drops into the Eel River valley west of Poland, the land productive. The road straightens for a few miles as it passes St. John's United Church of Christ. The map notes two towns along the road, but we see no markers for either Stealeyville or Prairie City. On the road is a fenced and gated home on a lake, an indication that not all opulent mansions are near major cities or in exclusive suburbs.

Ind. 42 meets north-south Ind. 59 just south of the I-70 interchange. Convenience stores are on each corner. Terre Haute is sixteen miles to the west.

To the west the land is flat for a time before Ind. 42 crosses over I-70 and runs past depleted coal fields. Clay County ends, Vigo County begins. Rural homes blend with farms. A small grocery is at roadside not far from Ind. 342 which leads south to facilities of the Indiana Air National Guard and Hulman Field, also known as Terre Haute's international airport.

Ind. 42 ends, as inauspiciously as it begins, at Ind. 46, which runs north and south along the far east edge of Terre Haute. There are few indications we are near a city of 60,000 residents.

West To East

Terre Haute to Ohio Line

Ind. 46 begins at U.S. 40, the National Road, at the east edge of Terre Haute and runs southeast across south central Indiana to the Ohio line. It bisects Spencer, skirts the edge of Bloomington, eases through Columbus and Greensburg and ends at U.S. 52 two miles from the Ohio border.

*   *   *

From U.S. 40, Ind. 46 heads due south and runs under I-70 before turning southeast past small farm fields broken at times by commercial enterprises. Near the town of Riley, Ind. 159 starts its route to the south; Ind. 46 continues southeast.

RILEY

The Past Is Present

Riley, divided by Ind. 46, is a town that appears bigger than its population, counted as 160 in 2000 by census takers. That likely is because the area is a suburb of Terre Haute, making the town limits difficult to identify.

Riley once had its own identity, its own role in Indiana's commerce. It was a trade center known as Lockport after the Wabash and Erie Canal opened and freight passed through locks in the area. The town was renamed Riley to avoid a conflict with Lockport, another canal town in Carroll County.

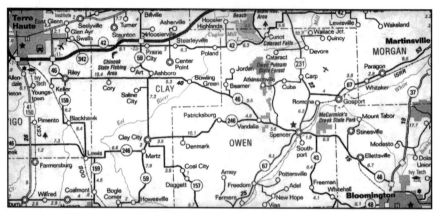

Riley also had a sobriquet. "Battle Row," some people called it for the melees that erupted among the European immigrants who helped build the canal.

The canal didn't last much longer than the fights. Trains came, rails rather than water carried freight, and Riley became a quiet town surrounded by farms.

Hints of the locks remain. Elementary students attend class in a school on Canal Street. If there is a street called Battle Row we do not find it.

Some businesses remain in town. Open are a food market, a coin laundry, other retail outlets and an impressive community center. Among the restaurants is one called The Life of Riley Grill.

East of Riley, Vigo County ends and Clay County begins.

CORY

About Those Apples

Orchards around town are now grain fields but Cory's heritage as an apple center remains. "Home of the Apple Festival," notes a sign at the entrance to Cory, a half mile south of Ind. 46.

The event held each September is a reminder of the mid-1900s when 280 acres of orchards in the area yielded 60,000 bushels of 35 different varieties. The orchards were sold after owner E. A. Doud died in the 1960s, the trees uprooted and the land planted in wheat, corn and soybeans.

Cory the town, however, has nothing to do with the center of an apple. It was named for Simeon Cory, a Terre Haute pioneer and hardware merchant who was so flattered by that recognition he paid for a town pump and the first school.

A marker notes the location of the Perry Township High School, home of the Apple Boys who won a sectional basketball championship in 1947. And who knows? It could have been the Cory cheerleaders who came up with the yell of that era:

> *"Eat an apple,*
> *Give 'em a core,*
> *Come on team,*
> *Let's score."*

Near the marker is a miniature park with three flag poles, which honor the nation, the state and emergency medical workers.

Like the orchards, the basketball teams are only memories. Students from Cory now attend high school at Clay City.

Gone, too, is the railroad. It also is remembered. A railroad crossing sign is posted at The Depot, a tiny ice cream shop where ice cream, milkshakes and sundaes are available in warm months.

It is one of a few businesses in town. McCullough Feed and Grain serves farmers in the area. The post office remains open in the unincorporated town so geared to agriculture a farmer marks his lane with a green and yellow "John Deere Road" sign.

*   *   *

Rich farm land continues east of Cory past the Hoosier Hills Golf Course to Ind. 46's intersection with north-south Ind. 59. The Country Junction Restaurant is at one corner, a manufactured homes lot at another.

Ind. 46 drops into the Eel River Valley before it rises toward the community of Bowling Green.

BOWLING GREEN
History by the Bushel

A huge historical billboard that looks like two pages of an open book is at the west entrance to Bowling Green. Called the Clay County Memorial Tablet, it notes the history of the area that was the first settlement in Clay County.

Bowling Green, which began as a trading post, was founded as a town in 1827 when it became the Clay County seat of government. A courthouse might still be on the old square in town had not someone sneaked into Bowling Green on the night of January 25, 1877, and moved the records by horse and buggy to Brazil.

Log cabin in Bowling Green

The cabal helped bring growth to Brazil, which remains the Clay County seat. The move left Bowling Green residents to share the town's pioneer history with visitors at its Old Settlers Reunion each August. One story they tell is about David Thomas, the first settler in the area. Thomas it is said, swapped two bushel of corn with the Indians for land on the bluff over the Eel River that would become Bowling Green.

The old courthouse was used for meetings until it was destroyed by lightning in 1910. The original steps from this 1853 structure remain on the east side of the square. A community center is in a brick building across a street from the square.

A historic two-story log cabin, built in 1864, sits across the street at the northwest corner of the square. A brick county jail near the square, completed in 1865, is now privately owned.

Some buildings like the old Village Mercantile are closed, unable to compete with giant chain stores in bigger towns. Still open, however, are the Bowling Green Market, two restaurants and one or two other businesses. The Wagon Wheel Inn serves meals; the other appears to be a stop for coffee and donuts. Neither has public restrooms, visitors are advised.

Hidden from Ind. 46 to the north is the Co-op farm service center and a church at Franklin and Jefferson that appears to be almost as old as the town.

The Bowling Greens of Indiana are like some senior citizens. Their past is vivid. Their futures are uncertain. As long as there are folks to attend the Old Settlers Reunion, Bowling Green will remain a part of the state's history.

*   *   *

Ind. 46 continues its southeast route 16 miles toward Spencer. It is a scenic drive, trees ringing the horizon. Clay County ends and Owen County begins. The terrain rises and falls, the road lined by woodlands and small farms. Hills and hollows allow dams to create numerous small ponds on farms.

Only one hamlet, Vandalia, its boundaries undefined, is on the route. A housing development called Hidden Valley Estates is off the highway near Rattlesnake Road.

SPENCER

Hot Dog!

Ind. 46 drops from its elevation into the White River Valley past a Wal-Mart, which, as elsewhere, has stripped downtown Spencer of many of its mom and pop stores.

Off to the south is Owen Valley High School, a consolidation of Spencer, Coal City, Freedom, Gosport and Patricksburg.

Ind. 46 joins combined Ind. 67 and U.S. 231 at the west edge of Spencer, creating heavy traffic as the congested roads ease east-west through town. Ind. 46 will not be a road less traveled again until it passes though Columbus 50 miles east.

Ind. 46/Ind. 67/U.S. 231, lined with businesses and fast food outlets, bisect Spencer. Many of the town's impressive old homes are to the north of the route. Its historic sites are to the south. So is the 1911 neo-classical Owen County Courthouse, a three-story limestone building with a brown clock dome topped by a flag pole.

A veterans memorial is on the west side of the square. A few feet away is the Spirit of America Doughboy designed by Ernest Viquensey, a sculptor who grew up in Spencer.

Railroad tracks run past the north side of the square. Across the rails are the three-story Union Hall building dated 1878 and other structures erected in the late 1800s.

The library and post office are on the east side of the square where parking spaces usually are open.

On this warm summer day, a hot dog vendor is ready for customers at his location on the square. Food carts aren't unusual in major cities. They are rare in towns with only 2,508 residents. For those who prefer more than a wiener on bun, the Chambers Restaurant, a popular smorgasbord, is just off the square. It is an eatery of choice for locals and a dining destination for area residents

A block east of the square is the 1855 Robinson House. Now called the Civic Center, it has space for a community center and a "fine gifts and antiques" shop.

Other historic homes are numerous, all within walking distance for motorists who need a respite from the fuel emissions on the road through town.

*   *   *

At the east edge of Spencer, Ind. 46 continues east. Ind. 67 and U.S. 231 turn north. A short distance ahead, Ind. 46 crosses White River and ascends a hill topped with an entrance to the north into McCormick's Creek, Indiana's first state park. Its hiking trails lead through canyons faced with high cliffs and limestone formations. Waterfalls cascade in creeks that cut through the park.

Overnight guests with reservations may stay in the Canyon Inn. Others may prefer to stay in cabins or pitch a tent at the camp sites.

Ind. 43 leads south just east of the park. Ind. 46 turns southeast at the Owen-Monroe County line before entering Ellettsville.

ELLETTSVILLE

Change of Identity

Ellettsville is another town that has had to redefine itself as its identity changed.

It once was a small town, its boundaries defined, its residents being neighbors with similar interests. That has changed. The town saw its population boom to 5,078 in 2000, a 55 percent increase over a decade.

It now is difficult to tell where Ellettsville ends and Bloomington begins. Ind. 46, which follows Jack's Defeat Creek (supposedly named when horses owned by a Jack Storm drowned in the swift current), is lined with businesses and shopping complexes.

Much of the road is being widened in this summer of 2001, which likely will bring more traffic . . . and more people.

Edgewood High School, which serves Ellettsville and Stinesville, is south of Ind. 46. An impressive library faces the road from the north side in what is the old business section of town.

*   *   *

Past Jack's Defeat Mall and other complexes, the urban sprawl ends. Narrow Maple Grove Road leads north a few hundred feet to a 180-year-old two-story home that is among the oldest in the state. Known as the Daniel Stout house, it is not open to visitors, but the native stone walls are said to be 22 inches thick. Trees, which appear as old as the house, shade the yard.

Back on the highway, Ind. 46 continues past the entrance to Hoadley Quarries, one of the major operations in what is known as the Limestone Belt.

Ind. 46 joins four-lane Ind. 37 at the northwest edge of Bloomington for a half-mile, then turns east as it bypasses the downtown district, which is to the south.

BLOOMINGTON

And I.U. Too

Informing readers about Bloomington is like telling Hoosiers about Bob Knight. Most people have stopped in the city, visited the Indiana University campus or attended athletic events.

Its population hasn't increased as fast as Ellettsville, but it did rise by 14.3 percent to 69,291 from 1990 to 2001. The result is continued development despite a decline in factory jobs lost to cheaper labor in Mexico and elsewhere.

Ind. 46 passes the I.U. football stadium and the I.U. Foundation facilities as it skirts the ever-expanding campus to the north and east. At Third Street, the road turns east. To the south is College Mall, which has been harmed somewhat by new commercial enterprises on the west side of town. To the north are restaurants and stores including a Barnes & Noble book outlet.

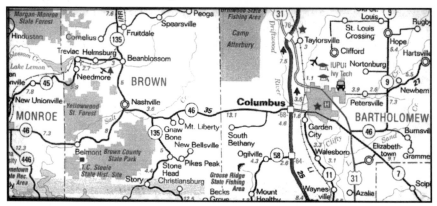

A mile to the east, Ind. 446 leads south over the Monroe Reservoir causeway on its way past Heltonville to U.S. 50. Two-lane Ind. 46 continues east past homes for four miles before it enters open areas en route to Nashville. Monroe County ends, Brown County begins east of Brummett Creek. At Belmont, a rural road leads south to the House of Singing Winds, which was home to impressionist artist T.C. Steele. The location is now a state historic site.

The road continually turns and twists; one of the rare chances for a motorist to pass a slower vehicle being a short straight stretch east of Belmont.

To the east Ind. 46 follows the Schooner Creek valley for three miles, passing north of Ski World and its slopes before turning northeast. Brown County State Park and its 20 miles of wooded roads and scenic overlooks are to the east where the road declines into Nashville. At the south edge of the Brown County seat, Ind. 46 turns east, joining Ind. 135. (See Nashville in Ind. 135).

Another entrance to Brown County State Park is two miles to the east. A short distance ahead, Ind. 135 turns south en route to its terminus at the Ohio River. Ind. 46 continues toward Columbus, 13 miles to the east.

Gnaw Bone Creek runs parallel to the road as it passes the settlement of Gnaw Bone, its antique outlets and tourist lures. Chances are the name Gnaw Bone has nothing to do with removing meat from bones. *Indiana: A New Historical Guide* notes that settlers may have called the place Narbonne for the city in France, the pronunciation evolving into Gnaw Bone later.

Beyond Gnaw Bone, churches, homes and farms are along the route that is usually heavy with traffic.

Brown County fades into Bartholomew County and farms reappear, then end as apartments rise to the south of Ind. 46 near a luxury-type Courtyard Motel. A shopping center is off to the north. It is obvious we have reached the outskirts of Columbus.

COLUMBUS
Athens of the Prairie

Ind. 46 crosses under I-65 at the west edge of Columbus where an arch rises over the road, a prelude to the famed architecture that gives the city "The Athens of the Prairie" label.

The road proceeds east, crosses White River's East Fork and enters downtown Columbus. It is best to park and stroll through the city's center, stopping at the Visitors Center, which itself is in a two-story landmark at Fifth and Franklin. Not far away is the city library, designed by Ieoh Ming Pei and Partners. The modernistic Commons-Courthouse Center, a civic center/shopping mall, is in the heart of downtown. More than twenty other gems of design are within a few blocks. Others are located throughout the city of 40,000 residents.

For those who prefer the old, the Bartholomew County Courthouse was built in 1874. It has been modernized and renovated over the years, but its French Renaissance design remains.

From downtown, Ind. 46 continues through the south edge of Columbus, turns southeast for five miles where it crosses old U.S. 3l, then shifts north for four miles to meet Ind. 9 at a four-way stop. Ind. 46 then resumes its route east. The hamlet of Newbern is just to the east.

NEWBERN

Bridge to the Past

Named for New Bern in North Carolina, Newbern is an old, unincorporated settlement established in 1832. As it was then, it remains a cluster of homes amid a few businesses, among them a flea market, antique outlet and garden store.

A park with a shelterhouse is near the United Methodist Church.

To the north an old steel bridge with a wood floor, itself a relic of the past, spans Clifty Creek.

*   *   *

Curves are numerous as the road angles to the northeast. One hairpin turn takes the road north, then quickly back to the east.

HARTSVILLE

All Is Not Lost

Small town. Big history. That's Hartsville, an incorporated town of 376 residents, whose past overshadows its present.

Two historical markers on the town square reveal part of its past.

One is about lost orders, the other a lost college.

Barton W. Mitchell's role in the Civil War is noted on one marker. It was Pvt. Mitchell of the Indiana volunteers and the Union Army who found Gen. Robert E. Lee's Lost Orders in a field near Frederick, Maryland, on Sept. 15, 1862.

The orders, which detailed Lee's plans for the Army of Northern Virginia, were found after being wrapped around three cigars, then lost by a Confederate officer. Mitchell passed the plans up the chain of command to Gen. McClellan, who is said to have asserted, "Here is a paper with which, if I cannot whip Bobby (Gen. Robert) Lee, I will be willing to go home."

Lee's lost orders may have helped the North whip Lee at Antietam, but it would be three years before the war ended and the troops could go home.

Mitchell is buried in Baptist Cemetery in Hartsville.

Another marker notes the founding of coeducational Hartsville College by the United Brethren Church in 1850. The school moved to Huntington where it became Huntington College in 1897, but not before its graduates became leaders in Indiana and throughout the nation.

A short time after the school moved, the college's main building burned.

Hartsville's square is unusual for a town without a county seat. Playground rides, a shelter house and park benches are on the grounds as are two well houses made of native stone.

A few businesses, including a liquor store and convenience store, are open, but the First National Bank, once in a 1904 building, is no longer in operation. A sign promotes the Volunteer Fire Department, the proceeds needed to help it continue to serve the area.

Large older homes are to the south of Ind. 46 near Jackson and Jefferson and College and Jackson, an intersection where an old pump, its handle still in place, is a reminder of the past.

A short distance east of Hartsville, Bartholomew County ends, Decatur County begins.

*   *   *

Farm land extends from each side of Ind. 46.

A sign promotes a Volunteer Fire Department fish fry at Burney, a small town to the north. Burney is another small

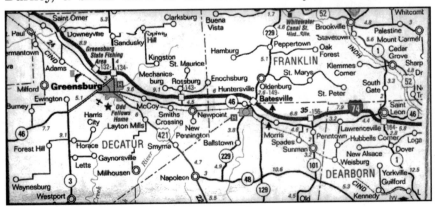

community that has seldom been in the news since its high school closed and the scores of its Panthers basketball teams no longer printed in newspapers.

A community of Forest Hills is off the road. Flag poles are for sale as Independence Day approaches.

South of a hamlet called Ewington, Ind. 46 becomes four lane and joins Ind. 3 for five miles. The roads turns east past flat farm land, then businesses, joining U.S. 421 for a short distance. A "Welcome to Greensburg" sign greets visitors near a Delta Faucet Company plant that is the city's largest employer. Ind. 46/U.S.421 enters downtown on Main Street, which runs on the south side of Courthouse Square.

GREENSBURG

More than Treetown

Tree atop Courthouse

If you're like most Hoosiers, you may think Greensburg is just a city with a tree atop its Courthouse Tower. Wrong! There is more to Tree City than a tree.

It's true the large-toothed Aspen remains an attraction as it has been for 13 decades. But it's not the only reason to stop in town. There's much more to see on a stroll around the business district.

The 1860 Courthouse itself is imposing, striking enough to have been cited by orator William Jennings Bryan as the finest example of Gothic architecture he had seen. The clock tower rises high above the two-story Courthouse, the tree the latest in a succession of Aspens that have been the city's focal point since 1870.

This Aspen looks healthy and vigorous, its roots anchored in the tip of the tower, its perch not as precarious as it appears. It is believed to be nourished by rain that seeps through cracks and sustained by soil and gravel left from the original construction.

The lawn below has its own history. It was the bivouac site for Union soldiers in 1863, the courthouse their temporary armory.

Businesses remain around the square, many on the street levels of three and four story buildings that date back to the 1890s. Many of the brick structures have cornices that project from the top; most appear well-maintained. On the square is an old-time hardware store, a far different—and more personal— place to shop than the giant Lowe's found in most cities of the new millennium.

Just northwest of the square is the Decatur County Historical Society Museum, its location once the K of P theater. The theater is believed to be the first air conditioned movie house in the state and the first to show movies with sounds.

A United Methodist Church is in an imposing building at North and Broadway.

Further northwest is City Hall, one of the most attractive in the state. On a triangle formed by Jackson, Center and Michigan Streets, it is fronted with steps and columns. Parking spaces on the streets are divided by flower beds.

A bed and breakfast is in a two-story building across the street.

Walking creates appetites. For the hungry, Storie's,

Greensburg City Hall

one of Decatur County's finest dining spots, is on the south side of the square. Spacious and neat, it offers a varied menu with an aroma of baking pies few visitors can resist.

Beyond the square, U.S. 421 departs to the southeast. Ind. 46, continues to the west, the street lined for a distance with older homes. Greensburg High is off to the north. The spacious city library with a huge parking area is near the edge of town. Off the road is the Odd Fellows Home.

Anyone who spends time here likely will agree that Greensburg is more than just a Tree City.

*   *   *

Outside Greensburg, Ind. 46, two lane again, angles slightly to the southeast. Lawns around some homes are huge, the grass green, neatly manicured. The road, lined with trees for several miles, parallels the railroad.

On the route is the village of Smith's Crossing; an antique mall, a repair shop and a few houses spaced between Ind. 46 and I-74, which is a stone's throw to the north.

NEWPOINT OR NEW POINT?
A Matter of Opinion

Don't ask if it is Newpoint or New Point when you stop in town. It might start an argument. The marker on Ind. 46 says it is Newpoint. So does the official state highway map. A sign at the post office notes it is New Point. So does our Zip Code book. As does our State Farm road atlas.

The name might be a good topic for discussion, but it's a Monday, a day when the Mid-Town Diner, the town's only restaurant, is closed. There's no one on the street and the postmaster likely is smart enough to avoid controversy.

The Mid-Town and the Post Office share the street level of a two-story building which appears to have apartments upstairs.

No one is at the town offices in what looks to have been an old school, or at the community fire department, which is run by volunteers. The car wash is vacant.

Down at the Wood-Mizer factory, workers are too busy making wood processing equipment to argue whether it is Newpoint or New Point.

A railroad cuts through town, but there is no depot with a Newpoint or New Point sign.

No matter the name, it's a small town of 290 residents, who likely have better things to do than engage in a spelling bee which might disrupt the harmony that otherwise prevails. That population figure, by the way, is from the 2000 census report for the town of "Newpoint."

Of course, the "New Point" folks are aware government has been wrong before.

*   *   *

Ind. 46 continues to follow the railroad as it heads east from Newpoint/New Point. A flat section ends and rolling terrain begins where Decatur County ends and the road crosses a narrow triangle of Franklin County. Ripley County begins a short distance ahead.

BATESVILLE

In Good Company

Critics sometimes call Batesville a company town. If that is true, it's not bad company to be in. That's apparent right off, just as soon as Ind. 46 rolls into town from the west.

Off to the north is impressive Batesville High School, home of the Bulldogs and the basketball teams that have given the city recognition throughout the state. Across the road is the Hillcrest Country Club and its rolling, wooded golf course, which is one of the finest in the state.

Ind. 46 intersects with Ind. 229 just south of the I-74 intersection at the north edge of Batesville. The usual cluster of fast food restaurants—and their constant traffic—create one of the few unattractive areas we will see around town.

Ind. 229 enters Batesville on Walnut Street where a banner acclaims, "You Can't Beat Batesville." The boast may be a slight exaggeration, but who wants to argue with home town pride?

Walnut Street reaches a T at East St. Louis Place, called that because it is the location of St. Louis Parish, its friary and the St. Louis Catholic School, which offers, a sign says, "Lessons for a Lifetime." The stately church has been a Batesville landmark since 1868.

Main Street, which also runs north and south, is a block east of Walnut.

The chalet-styled Sherman House, 35 South Main, has been a Batesville fixture since 1852, serving excellent food and providing quarters for overnight guests. Chances are your tour book will recommend both the restaurant, which offers elegant dining in a European-type setting, and the inn, which is a pleasant diversion from interstate motels on the Indianapolis-Cincinnati route.

Muggsy's Bistro at Walnut and Ripley offers food in a less formal setting.

City offices and the police station are downtown as is the Hill-Rom Training center. Which brings us back to why some annotators refer to Batesville as a company town.

It is here that Hillenbrand Industries, including the Batesville Casket Company and Hill-Rom, are located, providing employment for residents throughout the area. The casket company's product is obvious; Hill-Rom makes beds, furniture, prenatal-neonatal and other clinical care products.

The Hillenbrand family has been a contributor to the Batesville economy since 1870. Its businesses, Hillenbrand Industries, continue to be the heart of southeast Indiana's economy. Its shares are traded on the New York Stock Exchange.

Most of the Hillenbrand production facilities are off Ind. 46 as it exits Batesville to the east. They, too, reflect the pride of that "You Can't Beat Batesville" sign back in town.

MORRIS

Third Century

Morris is a small town east of Batesville, its focal point a spire that reaches toward the heavens from St. Anthony Church, circa 1885. The church school next door dates back to 1917.

A walking trail is near the church, which is fronted to the south by a park-like setting.

Two apartment buildings, each with multiple units, are nearby. The town has its own post office despite its nearness to Batesville. A day care center and a lawn and garden center are on Ind. 46.

*   *   *

Back on Ind. 46, newer homes blend with older two-story bricks from an earlier time. A convenience store, a recreation center and a golf cart rental outlet are ahead. It is an area near a popular recreation area that includes the Indian Lakes Golf Course and the Indian Lakes Wilderness.

PENNTOWN
Elvis Lives

Penntown isn't too much bigger than the four-way stop at the intersection of Ind. 46 and Ind. 101. I-74 is just a mile to the north. A convenience store at the crossroads is the town's only business.

Among the few houses is the century-old St. John's United Church of Christ. A new addition indicates growth in the congregation. An old cemetery covers a slope behind the church. Less than two blocks away is the yellow brick Baptist Church of Pipe Creek, circa 1884, which also has a graveyard on its grounds.

Still open, as it has been for decades, is the Old Brick Tavern with two benches out front on the porch. Chances are the seats were used by those waiting for the chicken dinners that made the tavern famous a decade ago.

A jokester has labeled a street as "Elvis Presley Boulevard." A bridge over a ravine next to the street leads to a home decorated with hanging baskets of flowers.

*   *   *

Ind. 46 continues east from Penntown, the road rising and falling over a rolling terrain. Ripley County ends, Dearborn County begins. Farm lands have all but disappeared. We are in the hilly, wooded area not far from the Ohio River.

LAWRENCEVILLE
Ghost of the Past

A ghost from a chapter of Lawrenceville's past remains, not far from a sign that points to its future.

"Closed" reads a sign outside the charred remains of the Schoettelkotte General Store, which promised—and delivered—"service with a smile since 1927." The store never reopened after a fire in the mid-1990s. A part of the town's history was lost and a reminder of the past was erased for generations yet to come.

Schoettelkotte's was no ordinary store. It was one where customers could ease through cramped aisles, past groceries, pop and candy and look at the clothing, bug spray, shoes, seed potatoes, wood stoves, stove pipes, garden supplies, horse collars, harness, nails, hardware, shovels, rakes, nuts, bolts, buckets, mail boxes, axes, saws and cant hooks.

It was a busy spot, one where motorists from Indianapolis, Cincinnati and other cities enjoyed a return to the general store of their youth.

Fire not only closed the store. It removed a point of pride for residents of the town founded in 1835 by John Lawrence. Only two or three small businesses remain. What was a town tavern is now the Door of Hope Worship Center, the name of the crushed stone street out front changed from Tavern to Temple.

A rebirth may be in Lawrenceville's future. Now open for development is Lawrenceville Farms Subdivision, "natural gas, city water, lots one acre or larger." Homes may replace the farm that once extended from a two-story brick home that remains on the site.

Cincinnati is within commuting distance and a few homes already are under construction. No matter how much the town grows, Schoettelkottes will remain a part of the town's past.

*   *   *

Ind. 46 passes over Ind. 1 south of St. Leon (see Ind. 1) and now runs north of I-74. The road declines through wooded areas as it drops into the Ohio River valley. There is little traffic. Two ancient I-frame stone houses are off the road. Trees line much of the terrain and the view is awesome in the fall when leaves turn from green into a multitude of colors.

Ind. 46 crosses over Whitewater River and ends at its junction with U.S. 52. It is just two miles to the Ohio border.

It has been a journey across Indiana, through cities and towns, farm lands and forests, reflecting the changes from the west to east across the state.

INDIANA
18

West To East
Across the State

On an Indiana road map Ind. 18 looks like a straight line to monotony.

It isn't. It is a route across the Grand Prairie and its rich farm land, past reminders of the Erie Canal, through small towns and the industrial city of Marion.

One mile may look like another at times, but there are secrets hidden at stops along the two-lane route.

Ind. 18 begins inauspiciously two miles west of Ind. 67 at the Illinois state line. There is no welcome to Indiana sign, only a 0 mile marker. Two young pheasant ignore our presence as they search out a late breakfast on the grassy shoulder. An old bungalow is the first house on the route.

A short distance to the south is Freeland Park, a farm town with a few houses now void of business. Gone is the Freeland Park High School and memories of its 1940 and 1941 basketball teams that were among the final 32 in the state tournament.

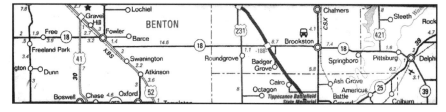

Two miles from Ind. 71 is what remains of the town of Free. It now is a railroad crossing with a huge grain elevator. A string of railroad cars is at a siding, perhaps waiting to be filled with grain from the vast fields beyond.

Views open on the horizon, the fields broken only by drainage ditches. Farm houses, mostly two-stories, are off the road. A short distance east Ind. 18 crosses four-lane U.S. 52, once the main route between Indianapolis and Chicago. Fowler is three miles ahead.

A historical marker near the road notes the New Purchase Boundary negotiated in the St. Mary's treaty. In 1818, the state acquired Indian lands that covered one-third of the territory that would become Indiana. The men involved in the treaty, Gov. Jonathan Jennings, Lewis Cass and Judge Benjamin Parke, would all have counties named for them.

FOWLER

Home Town Flavor

A church spire that can be seen for miles rises over the flat terrain. It leads to Fowler and the Sacred Heart Church and its school.

Fowler appears much like it has for decades. Franchise restaurants and chain stores are few. The Benton Café, not a Perkins or a Hardee's, lures diners to breakfast and conversation. There are no supermarkets, no huge discount stores.

High school students now attend Benton Central, a consolidation of what once were 12 county schools. Fowler is in the heart of Benton County, but it remains small, its population no more than 2,500.

A two-story brick, dated 1895, remains at the corner of 5th Street and Adams Avenue. A few other two-story buildings are in the business district.

An architecturally impressive Carnegie Library remains, yet to be replaced by a modern but unimpressive structure as it has in many towns. Due for renovation—and eventual reopening—is the 1940 Fowler Theater, another town landmark. It was saved from demolition by the Prairie Preservation Guild with an assist from the Historic Landmarks Foundation of Indiana.

Benton County Courthouse in Fowler

Large old homes are on tree-lined streets, among them the Ella Grant Lawson Home on 6th Street, now home to the Benton County Historical Society. The homes reflect the wealth agriculture helped bring to the county. Fowler is not like most county seats in Indiana, whose courthouses dominate the centers of towns. The courthouse in Fowler is on Fifth Street several blocks east of the town's business center.

Arched windows accentuate the imposing two-story brick and stone structure. A one-story addition reflects the need for additional space and the growing demands on county governments throughout the state.

*   *   *

Ind. 18 accompanies U.S. 52 a mile or so southwest, then turns to begin a 15-mile route due east to Brookston.

Ahead are mile after mile of ideal farm land, the soil rich as any in the state. Almost every acre, outside Fowler and smaller hamlets, is farmed. Homes are few, farms are large. Income per farm is among the highest in the state.

It was obvious as America moved west that the prairie was productive. Eastern investors saw the value of the land early.

Cattle barons followed, living, as *Indiana: A New Historical Guide* notes, "on a scale that exceeded the southern planter aristocracy." Times changed and farmers took over the land, giving it care the speculators and absentee owners did not.

Traffic is light as the road leads east past farm homes with tended lawns.

Benton County ends, White County begins. Ind. 18 crosses U.S. 231 just north of Roundgrove. A short distance away, the road passes over I-65 and continues east into Brookston.

BROOKSTON
Talking Bread

In Brookston, Ind. 18 makes a two-block jog south on Ind. 43 before again turning east.

Brookston's greatest asset may be its location. It has a rural town charm (population 2,000), but is within a 15-minute drive to shopping malls in Lafayette and West Lafayette and events at Purdue University. Fast food franchises and major discount stores have not yet reached the town to clutter its entrances or detract from its appeal. Most of its businesses remain independent. A grain elevator reflects the importance of agriculture to the area.

The Prairie Township Library is a fixture as it has been since 1916. Parks offer playgrounds for toddlers, ball diamonds for youth and shelterhouses for families. An elementary school remains. Frontier High School is a short distance away near Chalmers.

Homes are well maintained and many have porches, reflecting a time when summer evenings were spent outside.

Most of the town's commercial businesses are in the block between Ind. 43 and the north-south railroad. One of those firms is the Klein Brot Haus and its European style bakery. "The bread everyone is talking about," it boasts. It is a good place for travelers to stop for coffee and a favorite pastry and to view the giant buffet with a huge mirror that graces one wall.

*   *   *

Small towns end abruptly and farms return. It is this way at the east edge of Brookston. It is nine miles to Pittsburg. Ahead, the land becomes rolling as road drops into Springboro near the White-Carroll County line. Springboro is a general store and a few homes. A short distance ahead, U.S. 421 heads north en route to Monticello and Indiana Beach.

The two roads continue as one east into Pittsburg and Delphi.

PITTSBURG

Echoes of the Past

Pittsburg is a ghost of its past. Built with the optimism of a canal town in the early 1800s, its doom came with the arrival of the railroad and the Wabash River no longer was needed for transportation.

Only hints of Pittsburg's past remain. Two restaurants, the Landmark and Bresnahan's, are across the main street, now known as Towpath Lane. Just north is a marker next to an old two-story brick store that once was the center of a busy commercial district.

Much of Pittsburg's history is noted on the marker. The Great Canal Dam was nearby, bringing boats to the area and providing cheap water power which was used to capacity. A row of blocks between the main street and the river flourished, allowing Pittsburg to equal, if not surpass, neighboring Delphi in business from 1847 to 1856. Flat boats were built in Pittsburg and steamboats were moored for a time on its banks.

Saw mills, flour mills, machine shops, foundries, shoe cobblers and cabinet shops operated.

About the only business the river supports today is an outboard motor rental and a bait shop topped by an American flag.

Business waned as the canal's use dwindled. The dam was destroyed in 1881 and with it the canal, the water power and much of Pittsburg's past. Homes remain, many anchored on the hill that rises to the west, the echoes of a once thriving valley heard only in the imagination of the mind.

A reminder of Pittsburg's past

The Missionary Baptists Church with an ancient bell sits high above the river.

At the entrance to Delphi, across the Wabash River, Ind. 18 joins Ind. 25 for a short distance through the heart of the Carroll County seat. A "Welcome to Carroll County— Where Your Opportunities are Endless" billboard greets visitors. It is good to see a county where its towns do not compete with one another for economic development.

DELPHI

Alive and Well

Pittsburg's loss was Delphi's gain. Platted in 1828, it thrived when the canal opened in 1840, but did not perish with it. The city prospered when the Wabash Railroad opened in 1856 and continued to grow when the Monon Railroad followed in 1882.

One of the few Delphis in the nation, it was named for the ancient town in Greece, the site of an oracle of Apollo who was considered the god of sun, prophecy, music, medicine and poetry. The athletic teams at Delphi High School are the Oracles.

The vision of its founders remains for Delphi, unlike other small (population 2,500) county seat cities, appears to have remained prosperous. There are few vacant store fronts on Main Street (Ind. 18) in the downtown area or on the east side of Courthouse Square.

Scene in downtown Delphi

Some of the old three and four story buildings date back to the 1870s. All appear to be well-maintained. An impressive three-story structure that once was the City Hall remains on the Square, although municipal offices have moved to a newer building.

Men who lived in Delphi in the late 1800s were well lodged. The IOOF Delphi Lodge 28 on Main Street opened in 1880, six years after the IOOF Carroll Lodge was built in 1874. Both buildings remain, as do others, proof of the durability of construction of that era.

A Civil War Memorial is on the southeast corner of the Courthouse, a three-story limestone structure built in 1917. The Carroll County Historical Society is in the basement.

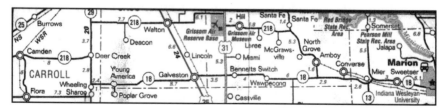

Delphi continues to make the old Wabash & Erie Canal a part of its present. A series of 12 trails with names like Towpath and

Millrace lead to old canal sites, the Wabash River and reminders of the mid-1800s.

The trails that follow along the canal are part of the Wabash Heritage Trail system that is open in a number of the 19 Indiana counties that border the Wabash.

Call Delphi a city where the past and present meet to shape the future.

*   *   *

Ind. 18 leaves Main Street and Ind. 25 in downtown Delphi. It turns south with Ind. 39 and passes Delphi High School. Three miles to the south it again turns toward Flora, six miles ahead. The land is fertile, the fields huge, the flat horizon broken only by scattered grain elevators and occasional wooded areas. Farms remain under family control, not corporations more interested in profit than the land.

FLORA
Proud and Independent

New homes, not clusters of unsightly fast food franchises, are at the west entrance of Flora, a farm town of 2,200 residents. A sign promotes Flora as the "The Garden Spot of Indiana."

It is soon obvious this is a quintessential Indiana farm town, neat, friendly, organized and independent with enough goods and services to keep residents from making trips to larger cities. It's small, yet big enough to bank, do some shopping, hire an attorney or enjoy a meal.

It isn't unusual to see a horse-drawn buggy with Amish aboard amid the auto traffic on narrow streets. Three two-story brick buildings marked E.G. Kitzmiller, with dates 1898, 1902 and 1909, are within a few hundred feet in the first block of South Center Street. Other structures have names and dates such as J. C. Winn, 1888, and J. H. Flora, 1895.

Things don't change a lot here. Step into the Corner Café at Main and Center Streets and you'll learn the old building has housed a restaurant for more than 90 years. It remains a spot where friends can gather for breakfast, engage in friendly banter

Business district in Flora

and debate the news of the day. One man's opinion counts as much as another's regardless of his station in life.

A few blocks north, Flora Seeds, reflecting the farm-based economy, occupies a huge complex.

Flora became a household name for Indiana basketball fans in 1946 when Bob Cripe and the Oyler brothers led the Badgers to the Final Four of the state tournament. It was the year Cripe won the Trester (mental attitude) Award, the event's top individual award.

Flora High, a victim of consolidation, is now a part of Carroll High School, its campus a short distance east of town on Ind. 18.

*   *   *

Carroll County remains flat as Ind. 18 continues eastward to the community of Sharon, which has a few houses and a Baptist Church. At Sharon, Ind. 18 merges with Ind. 29 for a short distance to Wheeling, which is another cluster of homes. Ind. 18 turns east. Carroll County ends and Cass County begins.

YOUNG AMERICA

A Bit of the Old

Used fire trucks, parked in a field, are for sale at the west edge of Young America, another farm community at the southwestern corner of Cass County.

In town, only a pizza shop appears busy. There are few other businesses. A gas station is abandoned and a two-story brick home that needs work is for sale. Chances are the town, like hundreds of others across the state, lost some of its enthusiasm when consolidation closed its high school. Homes, however, have been well-maintained as has a park at the south end of town. Streets are named.

A church now is marked as the Young America Lions Club. The volunteer Fire Department is in another building on the road. A post office, which is in an addition to a house, is a place for residents to network.

A sign outside the First Baptist Church offers advice: "Can't sleep? Don't count sheep, talk to the shepherd."

*   *   *

Farms, their fields as flat as a board, continue to line the road on its nine-mile route to Galveston. Only a gentle double curve interrupts its straight path. A farm is marked with the name of its owners. Harvestores and grain storage bins rise into the cloudless sky.

Traffic remains light as it has since the Illinois border.

GALVESTON

Vested Interest

Galveston, pronounced Gal-VEST-ton, is a community of 2,000 residents, many of whom work in Kokomo, a short distance to the southeast. It seems, to a visitor, more like a suburb than a farm town.

A sign salutes the Lewis Cass High School marching band. Little League diamonds and the Galveston City Park, with a community building, are at the west edge of town. Residential streets are shaded, the homes well kept. A portable basketball goal is at the edge of one street, the pavement at times used as a court.

Businesses are centered near Sycamore and Jackson Streets, but this does not appear to be a big shopping town. Its proximity to the giant chain stores in Kokomo make it difficult for individual merchants to compete. A lumber business and a few other retail outlets, however, seem to be busy.

A sign at the First Baptist Church in the center of town reminds readers, "A lot more could be established in this world if no one cared who got the credit."

It is obvious some people have done a lot for Galveston even if they did not get the credit.

*   *   *

Cass County ends and Miami County begins at the east edge of Galveston. Three miles east of Galveston, Ind. 18 crosses four-lane U.S. 31, the main link between Indianapolis and South Bend. A convenience store, a monument shop, a manufactured housing sales lot and a brick home are at the four corners. Kokomo is seven miles to the south on U.S. 31; Bennetts Switch just ahead on Ind. 18.

BENNETTS SWITCH
Lights, Action, Camera

"Bennetts Switch or Bennett's Railroad Station? Our Indiana map says it is Bennetts Switch. So do most historical references. A few call it Bennett's Railroad Station.

It's not much bigger now than it was in the 1800s, when trains switched here and 100 residents called it home. Those who chose to head north or south could take the train. Those who needed to head east could take the tri-weekly stagecoach four miles to Wawpecong for 40 cents.

The town now is a pleasant residential community with a bank branch and a business or two.

Bennetts Switch, however, is not without its heritage. It is the ancestral home of actor Richard Bennett and his actress daughters Constance, Joan and Barbara Bennett. He was the grandfather of talk show host Morton Downey Jr.

Bennett was a Broadway luminary before he moved west to star in such movies as "Arrowsmith," shot in 1931, and the "Magnificent Ambersons" filmed in 1942. He continued, according to *All Movie Guide*, to act until 1978 when he appeared in "Harper Valley P.T.A."

*   *   *

East of Bennetts Switch, the eight-foot high stump of a huge tree serves as a stand for the American flag. A 1914 barn, painted red, has dormer windows in its loft. A crib for ear corn and a chicken house also are red. It is a scene from the past when every farm family had a barn, milked cows, gathered eggs and turned what it produced into meals.

A row of houses breaks up the farm fields near Strawtown Pike, which leads north to Maconaquah High School. It is here the road makes two 90-degree turns as it enters Wawpecong.

WAWPECONG
Route to MIT

Like Indiana itself, Wawpecong got its name from the Indians who once populated Miami and other counties.

Today Wawpecong is four 90-degree turns on Ind. 18 amid nice homes in a pleasant pastoral environment. A gasoline station, the kind with a bay under a roof on one side of the pumps, no longer is in business. The pumps are gone as are most reminders of Wawpecong's history, which reveal a more prosperous town in the late 1800s. The land produced grain and the woodlands lumber for exports.

It, too, has its favorite son. Robert Schrock, as do most youths who grew up in a farm environment, learned the value of hard work, won a scholarship to Indiana University and became chairman of the Department of Geology and Geophysics at the Massachusetts Institute of Technology.

*   *   *

Wawpecong is wedged between farm land that extends in all directions. To the east three Harvestores tower above other grain storage units at one farm. Clothes dry on the line outside another home near a sign that points the way to a Mennonite Church.

Giant steel skeletons carry transmission lines from the north to the south over Ind. 18 to electrify both farms and cities. The road takes a slight turn south as it approaches Converse, a town at the southeastern tip of Miami County.

CONVERSE

The Taste of Indiana

Converse's business district is three blocks north of Ind. 18 on Jefferson Street. Old buildings, some with historic designations, are in the downtown area as is a Carnegie Library and a brick railroad station.

Platted as the town of Xenia in the mid-1800s, it was renamed Converse in 1892 by the postal service.

The town of 1,200 appears to be self-sufficient even though Marion and its discount stores are less than 15 miles away.

A must stop is the Herschberger Essen Haus, which we rated one of the top ten family restaurants in the state in our book *Main Street Diners*. Its breakfast menu is extensive. The "Sampler Platter" can nourish a working man for the rest of the day. For $6.95 it includes two eggs, one hotcake, hash browns, a half order of biscuits and gravy, two pieces of bacon, a sausage patty and coffee. The "Farmers Special" includes two eggs, hash browns, a half order of biscuits and gravy, grilled tenderloin and coffee.

Dinner meals include all you can eat entrees. Prime rib is a big favorite on Saturday nights. And if you're still hungry you can order a piece from one of "Ruth's famous home made pies" or the apple dumplings.

If that isn't enough, owners Freeman and Ruth Herschberger are nice people as are most of the customers who go there day after day or week after week.

Back on the road, Ind. 18 passes an old building marked "Auditorium," which was the Converse High School gym. Older basketball fans remember coach Dan Ballard's 1944 "Bordermen" who had a 27-0 record before losing in the semifinal round of the state tournament. Among the players was Bob Macy, an Indiana all-star who became a coach and is now in the Indiana Basketball Hall of Fame.

*   *   *

Miami County ends at the east edge of Converse and enters Grant County. Ind. 18 angles southeast and intersects at Mier with north-south Ind. 13. The Oak Hill United School Corporation offices are in Mier, which is a mere pinpoint on the map.

Ind. 13 soon turns north and Ind. 18 continues to the east. Oak Hill High School is in the northeast corner formed by the roads. Oak Hill is a consolidation of Converse, Swayzee and Sweetser, three old athletic rivals who now compete as the Oak Hill Golden Eagles. Sweetser is just ahead.

SWEETSER

Awake at the Switch

Anyone who does not deviate south off Ind. 18 into Sweetser is the loser. The town's spirit and enthusiasm is apparent in the old downtown area. It is there that the Sweetser Switch trail begins on the site of an abandoned railroad.

It is more than just a mile-long trail east, however. It is a tribute to the individuals and organizations that have contributed to it beautification. Small plots at the edge of the trail, planted in flowers and greenery, are being developed. Benches, donated by citizens, are in place and it is obvious the "Switch" is a source of community pride.

A railroad mail car and a caboose are on a short siding near the trail.

The paved trail is for biking, jogging, skating and walking. An unpaved trail can be used for horseback riding, mountain bikes and hikers. And when the Halloween season arrives, the walk is lighted by jack-o-lanterns.

Start of Sweetser Switch trail

A small restaurant is across Main Street as is the Town Hall. To the north is the 1922 Auditorium, which is now the Sweetser Lions Club community building.

Chances are land baron James Sweetser would be proud of the town he founded in 1871 and the 1,100 residents who now occupy its homes.

*   *   *

Ind. 18 parallels the trail east from Sweetser, then rises over an overpass where Marion's industrial complex begins. A recycling center is off the road as is the huge General Motors Metal Fabricating Division.

MARION

Pageants and Parades

Ind. 18 is one-way east as it eases through Marion's narrow streets and enters the heart of the downtown area.

On the street is the Grant County Courthouse, an 1880 classic revival structure. The Municipal Building is in the area as is the County Office and Security Complex.

A few blocks away rooms are for rent in the 1904 Grant County Jail, now called Castle Apartments. The impressive castle-like structure was empty for ten years before local government units bought the building with the help of the Indiana Historic Landmarks Foundation.

Crenellated turrets on each corner of the brick jail are now bedroom alcoves. Rentals allow tenants to live in a "cell" and enjoy the stay. Credit the landmarks group, Research Group Incorporated and the city of Marion for saving a part of history.

A cursory description of Marion is unfair. There is history, a college, huge homes and other attractions that take at least a day to see. It is suggested that a trip to Marion be scheduled around one of the city's annual events such as the famed Easter Pageant which involves hundreds of volunteers, the Ethnic/International Festival, the Quilters Hall of Fame, the Mississinewa 1812 Reenactment or the Christmas parade.

And a Friday night in winter is always a good time to watch the tradition-rich Marion High School Giants compete on the hardwood against a North Central Conference opponent.

*   *   *

From Marion, Ind. 18 becomes a divided four-lane road for seven miles to I-69. The interchange has the usual food and gasoline outlets for travelers. Ind. 18 continues east, Ind. 5, two miles ahead.

Fields and rural homes, occupied by families whose income comes from industry not agriculture, line the road. A spacious residence off to the side is fronted by a pond, park and shelterhouse.

Mailboxes are in various colors and shapes, one anchored to an old breaking plow once pulled by horses as its moldboard overturned the soil.

An overnight rain has freshened the air and the sun glistens on the dampened grass.

ROLL

The Cheering Stopped

Roll is another small town whose past exceeds its present. Automobiles allowed its residents to go elsewhere to shop and consolidation took away its school.

On this morning, a mother waits with her child along a street for school bus to arrive.

What once was Roll High School remains, but it no longer echoes with laughter of students or cheers for its athletes. Memories likely remain, however, from 1951 when coach Cletus Johnson and his Red Rollers won the school's only basketball sectional championship.

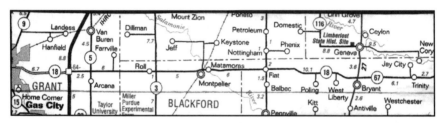

The high school closed in 1962, the students sent down Ind., 18 to Montpelier, which itself would be incorporated into Blackford High in 1969.

A two-story frame building that appears to once have been a general store and later a restaurant is closed, a "For Sale" sign's posted.

Most homes, however, appear well-maintained. An attractive newer one faces a small lake overlooked by statues of deer.

Times change, but community pride continues.

*　　*　　*

A short distance east, Ind. 18 crosses Ind. 3. A gift gallery and ice cream and sandwich shop are at one corner, farms on the other three. The town of Montpelier is five miles ahead.

MONTPELIER
Proud and Statuesque

From the first impression to the last, it's easy to like Montpelier. For a city of 2,000 there is much to see and a lot to admire. It is a place to stroll the downtown area, admire the architecture that remains and read the advertisements for local business that adorn the brick walls of historic buildings.

It has a sense of pride often missing from small communities.

Statue marks the Godfroy Indian Reserve

Except for a state capitol building, it has as many attractions as the capital of Vermont for which it was named. At least three parks are in town, so are numerous businesses that occupy most of the store fronts near Huntington and Main Streets in the heart of town.

Abel Baldwin brought the name Montpelier with him when he came to the area from New England and platted the town in 1837. Exactly 50 years later, oil was discovered in what was called "the best oil field east of the Mississippi." Montpelier prospered. Marathon Oil soon opened an office and construction started on many of the two and three-story buildings that remain.

It no longer is called "Oil City" and many of the horses are gone from the pastures that made Montpelier the center of harness racing on the "fast" clay track that remains in use.

Oil was depleted, but Montpelier still prospers when other small towns strive for survival.

A 25-foot statue towers above the main intersection, a reminder of the Indians who once occupied the area. A marker at the memorial notes the Godfroy Reserve, a 3,840-acre site (three miles to the east) that was set aside in the 1818 Treaty of St. Mary's with Francois Godfroy, chief of the Miami Nation of Indiana.

A grade school remains in Montpelier, but high school students attend Blackford High School north of Hartford City.

A sizable cemetery shaded with old trees, the grass trimmed, is at the east edge of town. Visitors would expect such attention after having seen the care given the rest of Montpelier.

*   *   *

The community of houses called Metamoras is at the edge of Montpelier. A wooded area is one of a few on this road across the state's farm land. Blackford County ends, Jay County begins and the fields resume.

At Ind. 18 and Ind. 1 is Fiat, which appears to be an intersection only. An abandoned church, a restaurant, a beauty salon and a gift shop are at the corners. A few Amish farms are ahead as the fields become rolling. Horses graze on pastures, the land too wet to work on this spring day.

Off to the south are the communities of Poling, once the home of the Poling High School "Polecats," and West Liberty.

Ind. 8 crosses U.S. 27 at the north edge of Bryant, businesses at each corner of the intersection. At a convenience store, a trailer is loaded with farm relics that date back to the early 1900s. The items include hand-operated corn shellers, seed cleaners and one cylinder gasoline engines—"one lungers" they were called. They are five times older than the young driver from Michigan, who is headed for a swap meet in Portland, seven miles to the south.

Ind. 18 ends at U.S. 27. Ind. 67, which has accompanied U.S. 27 from Portland, turns east and continues on to the community of Trinity and the Indiana-Ohio border.

EAST TO WEST

Portland to Pine Village

Ind. 26 extends across the state, ten miles or so south of Ind. 18. It, too, passes through small towns, historic sites and rich soil. The terrain, too, is level, except for some hills south of Upland and east of Lafayette.

The road begins at the state line where Ohio 119 ends. It sweeps gently to the north, passes the old Noble Township school, eases through residential Bellfountaine, then heads due west to Portland. Farms and homes on small lots are along the road as are a few wooded areas.

PORTLAND

"Egg Citement"

Visitors to this Jay County seat are greeted by the Chamber of Commerce with "Welcome to Portland - A Place to Grow" signs. Ind. 26 narrows as it enters the city from the east and passes old Portland High School and the Jay County Boys Club Community Center.

Portland's history is much like other cities in east central Indiana. Like them, its boom came in the late 1800s when gas wells brought industry and workers who made the city home.

When the gas supply dwindled in the early 1900s, the population growth leveled off and industry diversified.

It is now a city of 6,437 residents with small factories and a string of businesses on Meridian Street, which doubles as Ind. 67 and—for a few blocks—Ind. 26. A block off Meridian on Main is the 1916 Jay County Courthouse, a two-story limestone structure with a dome over a marble-floored center where stairways, also marble, lead to the second floor.

At the east side of the courthouse, both sides of a narrow street are lined with cars, leaving just enough room for another vehicle to ease past. Even small cities can have a shortage of parking.

Near the courthouse, "Shrek," the kids' movie, is playing. The theater remains a fixture in the downtown area, not yet replaced by a multi-screen complex often seen at the edges of similar size cities.

An Arby's, a McDonald's and a Village Pantry are along the main route through the city, but the real Portland is found at Kate's Coffee Shop at 224 South Meridian. Kate's isn't a fast food outlet, far from it. It's old-fashioned dining, the kind that takes you back to the small town restaurant of the 1940s.

With good reason. A diner has been a fixture at the same location since 1944; the name a memorial to Kate and Charles Thorn who ran it for five decades.

It is 7 a.m. and four couples, all from town, are seated near the front door. They are dining on owner Ruth Bruss' breakfast amid a continual conversation at what is called "the big bullcrap" table. "You almost need hip boots to walk through the stuff," the congenial owner told us on an earlier visit.

It is not unusual for customers to be waiting when the door opens at 5 a.m. In addition to the merriment they are there for the food for which Ruth is noted. The "Egg Citement," for example, offers eggs and a variety of options. Ham and cheese omelets are favorites as are the waffles.

Luncheon entrees vary by the day, meatloaf, chicken dumplings and beef and noodles, all with a home cooked flavor the fast food outlets up the street do not have. Kate's is open until 2 p.m. weekdays and until 10 a.m. on Saturdays.

*   *   *

Ind. 26 remains narrow as it leaves Portland to the west. Off the road is Jay County High School, a consolidation of Portland, Bryant, Dunkirk, Madison Township, Gray, Pennville, Poling and Redkey.

Beyond, trees form boundaries between farms. The road makes a 90-degree turn north for one-half mile before abruptly turning due west.

The Walnut Grove Church and a cemetery are at a country crossroads called Center. If Center had a past it is stored only in the memories of those who lived there.

Outbuildings at some farms along the route are in need of repair. For farmers, attention to the land and to the crops comes first, buildings second. Other farms are dotted with numerous grain storage units. At Ind. 1, Ind. 26 turns north for a half-mile then again makes a turn to the west. Jay County ends, Blackford County begins. The road remains narrow. Off in a lot, 13 giant work horses graze on the damp grass. They are reminders that some farmers still prefer to use real horsepower, not mechanical monsters, to till the land.

A road sign identifies Trenton. It's so small the speed limit drops from 55 to just 50. A cemetery and 20 or so houses—but no businesses—are between the Trenton signs.

Amid the farms at County Road 500 East is the Blackford County Security Center, a politically correct term for a jail and the sheriff's headquarters. Nearby an old frame home is accentuated with a small park, proof that homes are what their occupants make them. It is not necessary to have a mansion to live a prideful life.

Not far from Hartford City an old school has been converted to a home.

HARTFORD CITY

Victim of Sprawl

Ind. 26 is narrow as it enters Hartford City from the east past old homes shaded by giant oaks and scattered sycamores.

It is soon obvious Hartford City, population 6,928, is emblematic of the problems faced by small towns at the dawn of the millennium. Many of its businesses have moved from downtown to out north on Ind. 3.

Downtown is a shell of what it once was when each store front was occupied and the Courthouse Square was a place for Blackford County residents to shop throughout the week and for young people to congregate around the square on Saturday nights.

Blackford County Courthouse

The Square was the center of town, a focal point, a place in which residents took pride. And with good reason.

The 1893 Courthouse, still towers over downtown, still one of the most impressive in the state. Its clock tower rises 160-feet over the three-story stone edifice built with stone and shaped by its Richardsonian Romanesque architecture. Columns round out the corners, and a metal roof covers the well-maintained edifice which is a national historic landmark.

Some older structures such as the 1890 Tyner Building and the 1901 Campbell Building remain as reminders of the time when gas spurred economic growth and made Hartford City a thriving community.

Change is evident on the square. Traffic lights still control traffic as Ind. 26 passes the courthouse. A block north, however, the lights remain, but do not function, leaving four-way stop signs to guide a sharply-reduced traffic flow.

Blame shoppers, not officials, for the change in Hartford City. When chain outlets and other stores opened out north along Ind. 3, the shoppers followed. As did those in cities across America, residents sought easy parking access, forsaking independent merchants for the pursuit of convenience.

Hartford City, however, has retained much of its industry, including its 3M operations, which produce a wide variety of industrial, electrical and specialty tapes as well as films and adhesives.

Ind. 26 passes the imposing Grace Methodist Church, nice homes and the Blackford Country Club as it exits Hartford City to the west. Farms appear not far away. "John Deere Lane" marks one driveway.

* * *

Blackford County ends, Grant County begins about five miles west of Hartford City. South of Upland, Ind. 26 turns south with Ind. 5 an intersection with a flashing red light. To the north on Ind. 5 is the town of Upland, population, 3,803,

UPLAND

University Town

It is soon apparent how Upland got its name. The town is on a rise, the highest point on the railroad that led to its creation.

It also is a town whose population is on the rise, up to 3,803 in the 2000 census, a 15 percent gain over 1990.

Much of the Upland of today, however, is not along the railroad, but adjacent to north-south Ind. 5.

It is there that Taylor University is located as it has been since moving in 1893 from Fort Wayne where it was founded in 1846. It is, however, a modern university and most of its attractive buildings have been erected since 1965. A 10-acre lake is on the hilltop campus that now covers more than 240 acres.

Upland seldom is in the news, reflecting the tranquillity of the town and the relatively quiet behavior of the Taylor student body.

*   *   *

Ind. 26 runs south with Ind. 5 for a mile before turning west again. The land is rolling, the setting pastoral, the drive pleasant. Suddenly the fields become larger. A four-way stop is at Wheeling Pike, a county road that connects Matthews to the south to Gas City to the northwest.

A marker at the northwest corner memorializes Trask and its importance as "a pioneer village that served as an important commercial, social and educational role for early settlers." Trask is no longer on the map, its role a tidbit for history.

Our drive is slowed by a torrential rain that makes visibility difficult at Ind. 26's interchange with I-69. A short distance ahead we take haven at a Campbell Farm driveway. This is a typical June cloudburst, a farmer's blessing for the moisture; his bane for any damage it may wreak with wind and lightening.

A mile ahead, a road leads a short distance south to Fowlerton.

FOWLERTON

By Any Name

This is a town of 298 residents that settled on its name after being known at times as Leach and Leachburg.

It was Benjamin Leach who founded the first glass factory after gas was discovered in the area. It was Elbert and Jeff Fowler who built a mill in town in 1895.

Among the glass products made in town were paperweights, which sold for $2.50 a dozen. They now are said to be valued by collectors and some have been on permanent display at the Chicago Art Institute.

The mill, the glass factory and the canning factory are gone. Fowlerton is now a quiet resident community perhaps best known for its annual Lion's Club tenderloin fry.

Ahead fertile land promises to produce bountiful crops for decades to come, not natural gas that led to boom and bust.

Across the fields four miles to the west is Fairmount.

FAIRMOUNT
Valuing Tradition

If Fairmount has a problem it is in deciding who to call its favorite son. Otherwise, it appears to be a prosperous town of 2,992 residents who live on quiet tree-lined streets within walking distance of the downtown area.

Main Street leads south from Ind. 26 past restored homes in the town founded in 1850. If any houses are unkempt, they are not visible. Community pride is obvious.

Surrounded by productive farms, this is a rural town with values as deep as the rich soil.

Businesses are clustered in impressive two-story buildings. Among them is a bank building, circa 1890, its door facing the corner, its cornices still atop the brick, its front accented by an onion dome. Other structures are almost as old. It is good to see the past does not have to be razed for the future. Not far away, the town library is in an old frame home, a fancy new building obviously not a necessity.

The Fairmount Historical Museum is in the Patterson House, a national historic site.

Back to those famous sons. James Dean, the actor, as in "Rebel Without A Cause," grew up on a farm near town, was a guard on the Fairmount Quaker basketball team and learned his first lines in high school. He remains, even in death almost half a century later, larger than life for his admirers. The James Dean Gallery is on Main Street.

Phil Jones grew up here, joined CBS and became a familiar face on its news programs before retiring in 2001.

James Davis grew up on a farm near Fairmount amid 25 cats and turned what he learned from them into the "Garfield" cartoon strip and a major business.

Their high school alma mater, however, is no more. Fairmount became a part of the Madison-Grant consolidation in 1969. We wonder if the three would have accomplished as much had they attended a larger high school.

Time your schedule for a long stop in Fairmount. You won't be disappointed.

*   *   *

Fine homes line the road as Ind. 26 continues west from Fairmount. The Wesleyan Campgrounds are off the road. A restaurant, used car lot and a farm home are at the Ind. 9 intersection.

Farms and fields stretch out from the road, which is now wider than back to the west. Traffic is heavier as Ind. 26 crosses Ind. 37. No businesses are at the intersection. The community of Hackleman is just to the west.

We will see few towns of size for the next 60 miles.

Farm houses, some with porches, a few with barns nearby. If farmers are in a financial squeeze it is not obvious.

Ind. 26 crosses Ind. 13 at Point Isabel, a wide spot at the intersection with a few houses, a volunteer fire department and a cemetery. A massage parlor off the road seems out of place amid the seed corn company signs.

Grant County ends and Howard County begins, one county much like the other. Hills are for southern Indiana. Flat land is for the northern section. The terrain extends endlessly to the west.

Five miles ahead, the community of West Liberty is a short distance north of Ind. 26. A small brick school, marked District No. 4 and dated 1897, is a reminder of the past. It appears worth restoration. An old pump, the handle in place is out front.

Across the road, houses line the two-street town, isolated and quiet. For those who abhor cities and noise, this may be paradise.

Back on Ind. 26 is another tiny town called Phlox, a word that can mean philosophic or phobia. We think of it as philosophic for there is little to fear amid two churches, 30 houses and an abandoned store that is in good enough condition for a daring enterprising entrepreneur to reopen.

A four-way stop controls traffic at the Ind. 26 and Ind. 213 crossing, which has farms at all four corners. An abandoned farmstead is off the road, which runs straight as it has since Fairmount.

At the Ind. 19 intersection, a farm market stand is closed, awaiting garden crops yet to be harvested.

Ahead is Hemlock, a community lined with trees, some of which may be Hemlocks. A post office is open to serve customers and provide a gathering spot for residents for there are few other places to meet on weekdays. A sign at the Friends Church reminds viewers, "If you flee from sin, you will not fall into it." A Baptist Church is to the south of the road.

Oakford, four miles to the west, is another bedroom community for residents who work in nearby Kokomo. The Fairfield Christian Church offers two services, traditional and contemporary, a trend among most denominations as they seek to serve a diverse population.

A golf cart business is in Oakford, which also has a post office, and two other churches. A housing development reflects the rural growth of communities near cities.

Ind. 26 crosses four-lane U.S. 3l, five miles south of Kokomo and its automotive plants and diverse industries. A service station is abandoned, but two other convenience stores remain open. New to the intersection is a CVS drug store. A meat market is in the area.

Houses follow Ind. 26 to the west past two huge churches, a golf course and apartments and townhouses. If there is a highway near a city, developers will follow it out of town.

"Quality Home Sites for Sale," screams a sign amid the farm land. Not all farmers want to leave, however, for their lives and hopes remain in the rich soil. One farm offers "rhubarb for sale," a surprise for those who never thought of rhubarb as a cash crop.

RUSSIAVILLE

Surviving Disasters

Few hints remain of a devastating Palm Sunday tornado that slashed through Russiaville in 1965. As did other Indiana towns, it overcame the devastation and rebuilt itself to remain home to 1,092 residents.

Russiaville had seen devastation before, once after a downtown fire in 1881, again when a 1937 conflagration destroyed businesses on Main Street.

Ind. 26 narrows between curbs as it enters town from the east and passes a grain elevator and a few businesses.

At the Town Hall, a sign promotes the Western Days Festival in June. In Indiana, it seems, almost every town has an annual event to give residents a sense of pride they can share with visitors.

High schools once gave towns like Russiaville a sense of community. Festivals like Western Days help bring residents together. What once were the Cossacks of Russiaville High are now the Panthers of Western High, a consolidation of Russiaville, New London and West Middleton.

At the Pit Stop, a restaurant in a small strip mall, we order the "Sweet Stack," assuming from the description on the menu it is a baked sweet potato. It is a sweet stack, indeed, a sizable pile of buttered and brown-sugared french fried sweet potatoes. It is a treat for anyone seeking a different taste in dining.

Russiaville was platted in 1845. Neither fires nor winds nor blizzards have stopped the dreams of the first settlers who called it home.

*   *   *

West of Russiaville the land remains fertile, the farm homes well maintained. Only a few small towns are ahead. Howard County ends, Clinton County begins.

Ind. 26 makes a slight turn, its first deviation in miles as it enters Middlefork. Not much remains in the community except a few houses and a frame building that once was a school. Across the Ind. 26-Ind. 29 intersection, an abandoned motel and restaurant are reminders of the mid-1950s when the diner was a popular stop for motorists who traveled the roads.

Cattle, the first herd we have seen on the road, graze on the lush grass of late spring. The land no longer is flat. The road rolls with the terrain as it enters Geetingsville, another pencil dot on the map. A church and a few houses comprise the town.

Ahead a barn is decorated on one end with a painted American flag, complete with stars.

Sedalia, another tiny community built along the road, has a post office with a roof that extends over the sidewalk. If Sedalia is like most towns, its post office is a community center, a place for residents to exchange news and share parts of their lives. A fan business, that appears to cater to farmers and their grain drying needs, is near the post office.

Hints of an abandoned north-south railroad are at the west edge of Sedalia, which depended on trains for its early transportation.

Just to the west, a two-story brick home is being remodeled. At the old farmstead, a silo is no longer in use and the barn and shed are empty. It, too, reflects the constant change in agriculture.

ROSSVILLE

Hornets Abuzz

Ind. 26 widens to four lanes as it enters Rossville past a golf course, a medical center and an antique mall. A four-way stop controls traffic as the road crosses Ind. 39 near the heart of town.

The Town Hall, fire station and one or two three-story buildings are in the business district. Some businesses remain, but others have relocated to the edge of town where parking is readily available. The search for convenience by shoppers has hurt the old downtown here as it has in almost every small town across Indiana.

The Rossville United Church, however, remains a fixture near the heart of town as it has since 1831. It is commencement time and a sign proclaims, "Praise goes for graduates who keep their wisdom and truths close to their hearts."

Rossville, population 1,513, has kept its high school despite consolidation and its Hornets basketball teams remain a source of pride for the community. Waitresses at Crail's Family Dining at the west edge of town wear "Hornets Nest" T shirts and pictures of some of the school's better teams are on the walls.

A supermarket and other businesses are near the restaurant.

*   *   *

Ind. 26 begins to curve west of Rossville and fields become smaller. An old farmstead is for sale.

A branch of Wildcat Creek crosses under the road at the east edge of Edna Mills, a town with a few houses. Auto enthusiasts may be disappointed if they stop at the Therapeutic Body Work. It is, we learn, a massage business which improves human bodies, not the looks of cars.

Just beyond Edna Mills, Clinton County ends, and Tippecanoe County begins. Pettit, a small town where each home seems to have a garden is a mile to the west. There are no businesses.

Fields become smaller and the road twists before declining into a valley where it crosses the Middle Fork of Wildcat Creek.

MONITOR

Small School, Big Memory

A decline in the road leads to the Wildcat Valley community of Monitor and its eight houses and one business, the Monitor Tavern.

Old high school in Monitor

It is its size or lack of it that made Monitor a familiar name to senior citizens who grew up as Indiana high school basketball fans. Monitor shocked the state in 1943 when its Commodore team upset Lafayette Jefferson and won its only sectional. It was Lafayette's lone sectional defeat in a 35-year period from 1937 to 1972.

Monitor High ceased to exist in 1958, but the school remains atop a hill to the north. It now is used by New Directions, its playground a storage place for pallets and other wood products.

The noise of saws now are heard where cheers once echoed.

*   *   *

Back on Ind. 26, the road rises and falls as it approaches the city of Lafayette. Houses now occupy a field where crops once grew. Not far ahead, ramps lead off Ind. 26 to I-65. The four corners of the interchange are lined with commercial developments, restaurants, motels, a Meijer Store and assorted businesses.

Urban sprawl seems relentless.

LAFAYETTE
Goddess of Liberty

Ind. 26 is lined with businesses as it extends west from I-69, then crosses U.S. 52 and becomes a part of South Street. Old homes line the street beyond the businesses as the road eases down into the Wabash Valley and downtown Lafayette.

This is a city with 180 years of history, much of which can still be seen in its old homes and its imposing structures. It is best to park and spend time in Lafayette. There is too much to see, too much to admire, for a stop-and-go look.

The Tippecanoe County Courthouse is in the heart of the Downtown Historic District on Main between 3rd and 4th Streets. The Courthouse combines a mix of architectural styles accented with a 212-foot dome topped by the Goddess of Liberty.

Blocks of buildings that have withstood floods and storm for decades can be found on walks downtown and in other historic sections of the city. Many are designed with grace and character seldom seen in the build-it-functional-and-quick architecture of the early 2000s.

The city of 56,397 residents, however, has not escaped the shift of stores from its downtown to shopping malls. The area around the courthouse no longer is a center for shoppers as it was in the mid-1900s.

There is too much to observe to elaborate on all that can be seen in medium-size cities like Lafayette. It is best for visitors to find what interests them. All should find whatever those interests are in Lafayette.

WEST LAFAYETTE
And Purdue, Too

Ind. 26 leads across the Wabash River to West Lafayette, home of Purdue University, which continues to expand on the high ground above the Wabash River.

One of 68 land-grant colleges, Purdue greeted its first students in 1874 and established its Agricultural Experimental Station in 1887. The Engineering Experiment Station opened in 1917. In the years since, Purdue has become a leader in agriculture, engineering, space exploration and numerous other fields.

The Agricultural Experiment Station and the various agriculture departments are south of State Street. The rest of the campus is to the north.

More than 35,000 students attend the university and its continual growth is reflected in the expansion of dormitories and other facilities to the west.

*   *   *

Nice homes dot the countryside to the west as Ind. 26 swings to the north before turning west. It is 18 miles to Pine Village, the only town on the road between West Lafayette and the Indiana-Illinois border. A white rail fence extends along the road at one farm as the land continues to angle to the northwest. A four-way stop interrupts traffic on Ind. 26 at an intersection of county roads.

Tippecanoe County ends, and Warren County begins ten miles from West Lafayette. The road runs straight west across the flat farm fields. Corn thrives in the rich soil. We have entered the eastern edge of the Grand Prairie that extends into Illinois. Barns are few, high rise storage bins numerous.

The absence of basketball goals are hints that the farm population is growing older. Sons of owners have left home to raise families, and there are few youngsters to shoot hoops and dream of stardom. If there were, it would be more difficult to attach backboards to round granaries than on the barns they have replaced.

PINE VILLAGE
Pineknots and Memories

Ind. 26 enters Pine Village, population 255, past a grain elevator. A Monon caboose rests on tracks in a small lot at Lafayette and Jefferson. Across the street, Ella's Café is out of business and some contents are being removed. A few businesses remain on the block that is Pine Village's downtown.

An elementary school is at road side. High school students now attend Seeger, a consolidation with West Lebanon and Williamsport. It was a merger that brought an end to athletic teams that were known uniquely as the Pine Village Pineknots. The Pineknots were seldom Havenots, winning six high school basketball sectionals from 1921 to 1972.

Basketball wasn't always the sport of choice. Doris Cottingham details in an Indiana Heritage Research report that Pine Village was a national power in professional football for two decades around 1900.

A fire station for the volunteer fire department is nearby. A woman greets the warm sunny morning by washing the windows of her home. This is small town America and neither maids nor cleaning services are needed to do work the residents can do for themselves.

Ind. 26 stops at a T intersection with Ind. 55 and turns due north. Just beyond the turn is Keith's Coffee Shop, which we mentioned in an earlier book called *Main Street Diners - Where Hoosiers Begin The Day.*

The Coffee Shop is still open and Keith remains on the job, dispensing coffee, food, soft serve ice cream and hospitality. Keith's is not a place for sophisticated dining. It's a man's place, a destination for farmers and other workers in search of coffee and banter as they greet another morning.

Every farm town needs a place like Keith's to replace the general stores, feed mills and barbershops of an earlier time.

A half-mile north, Ind. 26 again turns west, makes a few sweeping curves and passes through endless farm fields, the land rolling at times. Ind. 26 joins U.S. 41 for a mile, then resumes its journey west. The state line is nine miles away. Off to the south at the town of Tab, a grain elevator towers over the horizon.

At the Illinois border, Ind. 26 becomes Ill. 9 in a blend of two states that make up a part of the harmony that is the United States.

*   *   *

Ind. 26 is a drive through Indiana's heartland. It begins in a rural area at the Ohio border, it ends in the prairie at the Illinois boundary. In between it passes farms and fields, crossroads villages, proud towns, universities and historic Lafayette. It is a microcosm of the state.

South to North
Continual Change

One mile may seem like another on some Indiana roads. Ind. 1 is one of many exceptions. It may, better than any other, show the contrasts in the state's terrain and its resources.

It begins above the Ohio River and terminates at U.S. 20, ten miles from the Michigan border. The road rises and falls as it passes woodlands, curves jaggedly on routes carved by the White-water River, meanders through cities and towns, crosses rich farm land covered with bountiful crops, skirts metropolitan Fort Wayne and enters the lake lands of the northeast.

This is a road to enjoy scenery, savor history and appreciate the variety in the state's geography, its terrain and its assets.

* * *

Ind. 1 winds its way north from Greendale, part of the Lawrenceburg and Aurora triangle anchored on the Ohio River in the southeastern corner of Indiana.

Like its neighbors and the rest of Dearborn County, Greendale has seen rapid growth. Its population, now 4,300, continues to grow as metropolitan Cincinnati expands into Indiana.

Dearborn is the state's third oldest county. It was an entry point for men, women and families as they moved north and west to populate Indiana and the lands beyond. Many stayed, leaving legacies that remain two centuries later.

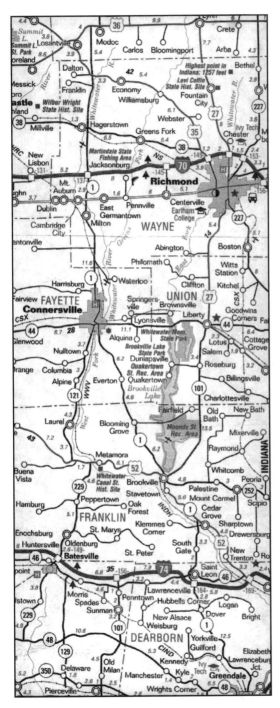

It is soon obvious Ind. 1 out of Greendale is not a straight-line road. It wanders around curves, searching for paths of least resistance on its way to the highlands to the north. It is not a highway for speed.

It is, however, a busy road despite its narrow, twisting route. Tour buses use it en route to the riverboat casinos at Lawrenceburg and Rising Sun. So do motorists who use it as a connection between I-74 to the north and U.S. 50 to the south.

An old corn crib built atop stones remains at a farmstead on the slope of a hill. The silo is unused, the farm idle. The land, though, is not worthless. Chances are a developer has eyes on it for a housing development.

A sign warns motorists to beware of deer for the next 12 miles.

Off the road is a horse farm. Not far away are ski slopes. Within six months the hill will be coated with snow, fallen or created, and packed with skiers.

GUILFORD

Vandals Beware

York Ridge Road leads to the west off Ind. 1 past a park called Covered Bridge. The name is authentic. A relocated bridge built by A. M. Kennedy in 1879 is the focal point of the site which includes a shelter house, playground equipment and grills.

Would-be vandals are warned they face prosecution. Covered bridges are a reminder of the past and need to be preserved. We

Covered bridge at Guilford

will, on this road, see other Kennedy bridges.

Across the road is the volunteer fire station, which promotes its benefit chicken dinner.

Guilford, an unincorporated town almost hidden in the valley of East Fork, remains much as it has for decades. There are few signs of growth or prosperity in the town itself. A row of old houses line the main road. The post office, painted blue and white, is the brightest building in the area. An old store is for rent, no longer used as a tire business or a general store, depending on the era.

An auto repair shop is one of the few businesses that remains.

Like many towns, Guilford lost part of its identity when the high school closed and its students sent to East Central High near St. Leon.

Some of the newcomers to the Guilford area live on York Road which ascends above the valley. Homes on the route are spacious and expensive, their views impressive.

*   *   *

Ind. 1 continues its long, steep incline from York Ridge Road on its way to Dover.

DOVER
In-SPIRE-ing

The spire of St. John The Baptist Roman Catholic Church rises high over the elevation, one of many steeples in the area that reach toward the heavens.

St. John's is the second oldest Catholic church in Indiana, established in 1814 in a log structure. The church in use now was erected in 1879. A pre-school and cemetery are on the grounds in the unincorporated village.

The Fischer's Bar and Grill, promotes its chicken and ribs despite a for sale out front. No other businesses are in town. Off Ind. 1 to the west, however, is Chateau Pomije, one of Indiana's better known wineries.

*   *   *

North of Dover, Ind. 1 continues to rise. A BP Convenience Store on the road just south of I-74 is busy. "It's always this way," an employee explains, noting the location is convenient for motorists on both Ind. 1 and I-74.

ST. LEON
Worth Crowing About

"Historic St. Leon," reads the sign at the entrance to the town just north of I-74 and Ind. 46.

Historic it is, for its church and for its tradition. As towns go, St. John's has never grown much since its incorporation in 1873.

Its 2000 population was 387, down from 493 in 1990, if census figures are reliable.

It is not necessary, however, to be big to have a place in history.

The church is St. Joseph Catholic, a parish established in 1841. On the church grounds, too, are a rectory and school. And a sign that reminds readers, "The 10 Commandments are not multiple choice."

The town's tradition is not only about religion. It's about politics, too. Chances are Andrew Jackson never stopped here. He likely never heard of the tiny town in northern Dearborn County. He would, however, have appreciated the heritage of his "Old Hickory" label.

Sign at entrance to St. Leon

St. Leon has maintained the only continuous presidential pole raising in the nation. A marker at the parish explains: "On this site since 1892, during each presidential election campaign, a tall hickory pole bearing an American flag and a Democrat rooster is raised by manpower alone. The once widespread custom dates from the 1828 campaign of Andrew 'Old Hickory' Jackson."

Residents claim a straight hickory tree is downed with a crosscut saw—not a chain saw—and all but a few branches removed with axes. It is then raised by manpower in a ceremony that includes a parade and speeches, political of course.

It is the kind of tribute even Republicans—moderate ones, maybe—can appreciate.

Anyone who wants to toast the pole raisers can do so at the town's only bar, which once doubled as a general store.

*   *   *

Dearborn County ends, Franklin County begins a short distance north of St. Leon. The road runs straight north past small fields in an area not noted for agriculture.

South Gate, a community along the route, is small; a few houses and a deteriorating two-story brick building. If there is a reduce speed sign, we do not see it.

A road called Wee Wee intersects with Ind. 1 near a big big hill that declines into the Whitewater River valley. Heavy rains have turned the river, noted for rafting, into a swift current. Ind. 1 crosses the river and merges with U.S. 52 on a northeasterly route toward Brookville six miles ahead.

At Mound Haven, the Mounds Family Restaurant boasts its fried chicken, ham and steak dinners. Small cabins and a motel are available for visitors who come to the area for recreation along the Whitewater.

To the north is the 1812 Little Cedar Grove Baptist Church, said to be the oldest Indiana church that remains on its original foundation. Some of the hand-hewn timbers and the original pews remain in the church now maintained by the Franklin County Historical Society.

The Franklin County Park, a mile west on Blue Creek Road, is a place to camp in modern or primitive areas.

BROOKVILLE
Rich in History

Ind. 1/U.S. 52 rises over the valleys as it curves past an attractive "Welcome to Brookville" sign then eases into town where the road flattens on the ridge of hills.

Streets in Brookville are not paved with gold. They are, however, lined with the priceless richness of the town's role in Indiana history.

It was here that pioneers and settlers came before statehood, some to stay, some to continue through this gateway to the land beyond. Those who remained built a legacy that continues into the 21st century.

It is Brookville that was home, at least for a time, to four Indiana governors. It was Brookville that helped give birth to the state. And it was Brookville that remained an important stop on the Cincinnati-Indianapolis route that later would become U.S. 52. And it was here, below the city, that the east and west forks of the Whitewater River merged to play a part of the state's emergence.

Franklin County Courthouse at Brookville

Three consecutive Indiana governors were from Brookville. James Ray served from 1825-1831, Noah Noble from 1831-1837, and David Wallace from 1837-1840. Abram Hammond was governor from 1860-61. Lew Wallace, son of Gov. Wallace, grew up in Brookville and became a Civil War general and the author of *Ben Hur* and other books.

Gov. Ray's home, built in 1821, remains just off Main Street.

To enjoy Brookville, it is best to park the car and walk a six to eight block stretch of Main Street (Ind. 1 and U.S. 52) where much of the city's heritage can be seen.

A historic area, part of which dates back to 1808, includes a cluster of well-maintained buildings that reflect the architecture of the 19th Century. Some are two and three stories; the upper levels mostly vacant. An example is the Franklin County Farmers Mutual Insurance Company, which is in an 1890 building that once was the Brookville Bank.

For a small town (population 2,652), there is a diversity of businesses. Real estate and insurance offices, a jewelry store, a karate school, a taxidermist, restaurants and other enterprises occupy lower levels of the old structures.

One of the most obvious, and newer buildings, is the 1912 Franklin County Courthouse, which is on a rectangular plot rather than square. A clock tower accentuates the brick Courthouse, which is listed on the National Register. Nearby is the County Security Center, known in the days before political correctness simply as the jail.

The modernistic Franklin County Bank contrasts the old and the new. So does a McDonald's Restaurant, a busy franchise that has taken customers from older restaurants. An ever-present Subway is across the Street.

Also on North Main is a Carnegie Library still in use after 90 years. Elegant old homes are a reminder of a more ostentatious time in small town society.

Not all Brookville landmarks are, or were, on Main Street. The side streets offer more reminders of the town's past. A marker on 5th Street near the Courthouse notes the Franklin County Seminary, which was open for two decades in the early 1800s. Another marker is at the site of Brookville College, which operated later in the century. The oldest church in town, home over the years to Methodists, Presbyterians, Lutherans and Baptists, dates back to 1821.

On the banks of the East Fork of Whitewater on 8th Street is "The Hermitage." The 17-room mansion with a 100-foot long porch was home at different times to T. C. Steele and J. Ottis Adams, two of Indiana's more noted artists.

All are assets that make Brookville one of the state's most historic towns.

*   *   *

Ind. 1 leaves U.S. 52 at the north edge of Brookville and begins its northwesterly route toward Connersville. The road twists through woodlands before the terrain flattens and farms appear. At roadside, fourteen sacks of trash at one home reflect the waste to which Americans have become accustomed.

The Fairfield Road entrance to Brookville Lake is at Blooming Grove, a hamlet with an old-time filling station, its pumps removed, its bays no longer in use. The 5,260-acre lake, the third largest in the state, is noted for its wildlife, its outdoor activities and its fishing sites. It also has been a revenue source for restaurants, stores and bait shops that cater to visitors.

A short distance ahead, Franklin County ends, and Fayette County begins.

EVERTON

The Cheering Stopped

Everton is among the towns that benefit from Brookville Lake.

A. J.'s place offers "fresh chicken and pizza" for sportsmen and campers. A bait and tackle shop has "tools" for fishermen. And chances are the day care center may offer to baby sit for adults who want a few hours of quietude.

It has been more than a half century since Everton had its own high school, but it's still possible to find fans who can name every player on its 1947 basketball team that won a sectional. It was a time when schools gave small towns a sense of community that consolidations do not.

Everton High closed later that year and students were sent to Connersville. And the town has been seldom in the news since.

CONNERSVILLE
All Aboard

Ind. 1 is marked Veterans Memorial Drive as it leads past old homes shaded with trees into Connersville, another city that grew up in the early 1800s on the banks of Whitewater River. No unsightly discount store or fast food restaurants detract from the view as the route leads to 5th Street en route to downtown.

It was at 5th and Eastern where John Conner, for whom the city is named, built a store and trading post in 1818. The structure remains as Connersville oldest business building.

Numerous downtown historic sites are within a short walk. The Fayette County Courthouse, built in 1849, has been remodeled to feature cone-crowned towers. Despite the changes, the basic structure remains as one of the state's oldest courthouses.

Fayette County Courthouse

The 1842 Canal House, in the 100 block of East 4th Street, features Greek architecture with columns out front. It was for a time headquarters of the Whitewater Canal Company and now is home of Historic Connersville.

Also downtown is the home station of the Whitewater Valley Railroad. It is there the scenic railroad begins its 16-mile route along the tow path of the Whitewater Canal. The road leads to Laurel and Metamora, then returns to Connersville. Anyone who wants to ride the train should check for days and times it operates.

Steel wheel baggage wagons are along the tracks, a reminder of the days when rail was the nation's main mode of transportation.

Large old homes line Central and Grand Avenues north from downtown.

On the north side is Roberts Park, its 100 acres used for swimming, recreation and enjoyment. A relocated 1884 covered bridge built by the Kennedy brothers is among the attractions in the park donated by Col. James E. Roberts in 1902 to the people of Connersville. Roberts was a Connersville merchant who moved to Indianapolis in 1893. Few cities with 15,411 residents have better parks than this.

On the north side, Ind. 1 turns west past a shopping complex, then turns back to the north. The exit from the city is less attractive than Veterans Memorial Drive into the city.

(NOTE: The author, a college student at the time, worked in Connersville one summer 50 years ago. Much of the city remains unchanged although more attention has been paid to preservation and history. The most obvious difference is the shift in shopping from downtown to the north side where parking is more convenient. Franchise stores and fast food restaurants have replaced home-owned businesses. Change is inevitable. It can also be regretful.)

*   *   *

Ind. 1 follows the railroad north from Connersville over terrain that continues to rise and fall, but more gently than the hills to the south. Two or three I-frame homes from an earlier era are on the road, one shadowed by oak trees that appear to be as old as Indiana.

Fayette County ends, Wayne County begins. Valley Grove Cemetery is on each side of the road that begins to twist as it nears the west fork of the Whitewater.

MILTON

After the Cheering Stopped

Anyone who fails to pay attention to small towns misses a part of Indiana's past and present.

It would be that way in Milton, an incorporated town of 611 residents founded in 1824 in the lowland near the Whitewater. It's a place to see clothes drying on lines, a basketball goal at the edge of Cherry Street, the pavement its court. And it's a town where some homes proudly fly Old Glory.

The youngsters who shoot hoops in town have heard—time and again—senior citizens tell about the time back in 1954 when the Milton High School Sharpshooters won the sectional. It was the school's only championship and it came in a tournament usually dominated by Richmond teams.

Milton, as did hundreds of other towns, lost its high school to consolidation. Students here now attend Cambridge City High. The school is now the Old Milton School Antique Mall.

The United Methodist Church has been a fixture in town since 1875. The Milton Christian Church is also here. A stoplight is on Ind. 1 and the Volunteer Fire Department is big enough to have three bays for its trucks. The Town Hall is in a small concrete block building. And Milton's Mini Mart is a place to stop for milk, ice cream and other supplies.

Streets have names like River and Canal, both of which have played a part in Milton's past.

It is in towns like this where the air is clear, the silence welcome and the clutter of metropolitan life non-existent.

*   *   *

Old homes blend in with new as Ind. 1 leads north from Milton. A short distance ahead, the road crosses U.S. 40. The National Road in eastern Indiana is sometimes called "Antique Alley" because of numerous shops along the route.

CAMBRIDGE CITY

Sisters Act

A short distance to the west of Ind. 1 on U.S. 40 is Cambridge City, another old town, neat, clean and historic. It is not advisable for anyone to continue north on Ind. 1 without stopping, because Cambridge City is part of Indiana's past and its present.

The town was founded in 1836, ten years before the Whitewater Canal reached the area. The Indiana Central Railroad arrived in 1853 and rails, not water, became the main source of transportation. Cars and trucks came later.

Anyone who doesn't stop will miss the Opera House, a three-story Italianate structure that remains. There have been no operas for decades, but the first floor remains in use. Also on Main is the Museum of Overbeck Art. It is a tribute to six Overbeck sisters, who lived in Cambridge City, turning pottery into art from 1911 to 1955.

Fines homes can be seen on Main and other streets in the town of 2,121.

And, yes, Cambridge City, is actually a town, governed by a Town Council, not a mayor. No matter! It's a nice place to stop be it a city or a town.

*   *   *

A short distance north of U.S. 40, Ind. 1 crosses over I-70 and the usual fixtures at interchanges. Each corner has been developed, each business dependent on revenue from travelers on the interstate.

Five miles ahead the road crosses Ind. 38.

HAGERSTOWN

Food and Thoughts

Hagerstown, like Cambridge City, is a must stop, even though it's off Ind. 1 a short distance. If attractions and history don't make the stop worthwhile, fine dining will.

It, too, owes part of its past to the Whitewater Canal, becoming the upper terminal of the water route to Cincinnati in 1847. But the Hagerstown of the 2000s is more than an end to a canal that soon failed.

It's a vibrant, clean town of 1,768 residents who can find much of what they need in local stores. A library has been here since 1863. Most buildings on Main Street (Ind. 38) are well maintained; the businesses varied. The newer Town Hall just off Main is an imposing brick structure, large for a town this size.

A three-story brick built in 1880 by the Independent Order of Odd Fellows is owned by Historic Hagerstown, a group dedicated to preservation and restoration. The lower level is rented by retailers, a museum on the second floor.

Unlike many towns, Hagerstown kept its high school in a consolidation with Economy and Greens Fork called Nettle Creek.

Ask most Hoosiers, however, about Hagerstown and they will mention "Welliver's." Welliver's is "that fabulous smorgasbord" at 40 East Main, which draws diners from throughout Central Indiana and from western Ohio. It offers dining in a pleasant environment. It's also a vast change from the gaudy Subway next door.

And there is humor in Hagerstown. A gift shop on Main Street is posted with witticisms. "If we don't have it, you don't need it," says one. Another reads, "Browsers wanted—no experience necessary." Notes another, "A penny saved does not add up very fast."

Life is not fast-paced in Hagerstown. It's a place where a man swings on his front porch while talking on his cell phone. You don't see that tranquillity in many larger towns.

*   *   *

Five miles north of Ind. 38, Ind. 1 crosses U.S. 35 before Wayne County ends and Randolph County begins. It is a fertile area and farms grow larger as Ind. 1 joins U.S. 36 for a mile to the east before again turning north.

Off Ind. 1-U.S. 36 to the south is Union Junior-Senior High School. A consolidation of Huntsville, Losantville and Modoc. The school remains small, enrollment usually around 150 students in the top four grades.

MODOC
Nice to Go Home To

Modoc is just east of the Union School, which may be its main enterprise. If 2000 census figures are correct, the town population is now 225. If there was a Chamber of Commerce here it would boast that it was a gain of seven residents over the last decade.

The nearest towns of size are Winchester, Richmond and New Castle, but no one seems to mind being away from a major city.

A loaf of bread or a gallon of milk is within walking distance to the Modoc Food Market on Main or the T & S Pantries store on Elm Street. So is the post office, where, if like most towns, a person can learn more news than from a weekly newspaper.

If one of the locals has a complaint, a member of the Town Council lives down the street.

It's not a bad place to return after a day at work in a bigger town.

*   *   *

Ind. 1 turns from U.S. 36 at Main Street in Modoc and heads due north, a route that will vary little for the next 10 miles. North of town, rows of junk cars are in an auto graveyard that could be called "rusthaven."

Oats, the first crop we have seen on roads in the summer of 2001, are ripening in a field that covers at least 40 acres. A herb garden is off the road in an area of farms and woodlands. The contrast in farmsteads is apparent; some well-maintained, others given little care.

Ind. 32 joins Ind. 1 for a mile before the roads enter Farmland as Main Street where neat houses are adorned with flowers that bloom in window boxes and baskets.

FARMLAND

A Restoration Textbook

Farmland is, of course, a farm town. It is, however is a model for villages and cities to follow in renewing historic landmarks and restoring vigor to deteriorating downtowns.

Call what has happened here textbook rehabilitation.

Farmland, population 1,456, reinvented itself through an organization called Historic Farmland USA with an assist from the Historic Landmarks Foundation and a Hometown Indiana grant from the Division of Historic Preservation and Archeology. Tax credits and private donations helped. So did support from merchants and property owners.

Old Mill Shoppes part of a "new" Farmland

Evidence of revitalization are obvious. An abandoned 1919 grain elevator near the railroad is being restored as the Old Mill Shoppes.

New businesses in the elevator and in other restored structures include the "Old Thyme Market," a gift store, art gallery, a stain glass studio called "Bright Ideas," a general store and a toy outlet. Icing is added at a dessert shop.

Under renovation is the four-story Masonic Temple, circa 1900. Parts of the imposing brick Italianate building, accentuated by a cylindrical corner, will be used as a community center and for office of Historic Farmland USA.

Other historic buildings are on each side of the railroad.

Downtown has become brighter as well as regenerated. A Red Gold Tomatoes mural, commissioned by the Red Gold company, covers an outer wall of the Thrift E Grocery.

This is not the Farmland of the 1980s. It is a town with its spirit refreshed. Yet, it seeks not to become a touristy stop in an effort to trap shoppers. The author of a feature story in *Preservationist*, a publication of the Indiana Historic Landmarks Foundation, asserts, "Our real goal is to share and celebrate the day-to-day lifestyle of the community with visitors." The unnamed author adds:

"The key in restoration is to keep the whole town informed. When everyone feels a part of the process it makes it so much easier to get the job done."

It is excellent advice for other towns seeking new images.

*   *   *

A mile north of Farmland, Ind. 1 turns west for a mile, then resumes its route to the north. Farms, woodlands and houses are along the road. An old store has been abandoned but a house nearby is being restored. A windmill spins in the wind.

BRINCKLEY
Boom Town

If a town is on—or off—the road, it likely has a story of its own. So, never pass up a chance to detour off the beaten path. You might never know what you've missed.

Take Brinckley, for example. It's a dot just east of Ind. 1 on our Indiana road map. The name is new to us. Nosiness and curiosity drive us in that direction.

We know when we arrive at a turn in the county road. "Now Entering Brinckley, Population 9," a sign tells us. "Joe Beatrice, Mayor," it adds. It is humor seldom seen in towns that want to exaggerate their importance.

Brinckley is a few houses and an abandoned store. No one is around for us to express our appreciation for the levity or to ask about its origin.

A few days later we telephone the home of "Mayor Beatrice." Lisa Beatrice, "Mrs. Mayor," explains that Brinckley was once a small town. "We pretty much bought the corner (the house and the old store) that had been the happening spot. The post office was in the store at one time."

About the sign? "Joe's boss had the sign painted and considered him to be the mayor of Brinckley when we moved here in 1989."

The population was seven then. It's now nine. A lot of towns would like to have recorded a percentage gain like that from one census to another.

"We've had several people stop and tell us what used to go on here. It's an old town that used to be called Shedville. The house is a hundred years old and the store (not in use) was here for years," Mrs. Beatrice explains.

"We hope to eventually use the store as a craft spot and maybe sell bread, milk and other basic items to neighbors," she adds.

That would keep folks in the community from driving five miles to Farmland. And give them and the curious who stop by a chance to visit with Brinckley's "First Family."

*   *   *

Nature trails lead off the road into Brinckley and a field at the corner of Ind. 1 appears to be in reforestation.

A farmer boasts he's a Purdue Boilermaker fan with a sign on his garage. Nearby is the Davis-Purdue Agriculture Center. Ahead, Ind. 1 crosses the Mississenewa River, the erect steel bridge painted a bright blue. The road then crosses Ind. 28 and soon enters Jay County from Randolph County.

The horizon opens, fields are larger, trees fewer. A cemetery is at road side. An old house has a metal roof, the kind that provide pleasure for the farmer when he hears the pelting of raindrops that soaks his corn and soybeans.

REDKEY

Nothing is Forever

Change is inevitable both for towns and for people. Redkey has grown accustomed to transition over the last 150 years.

Founded in 1854 as Mount Vernon, it was renamed in 1867 for Methodist minister James Redkey.

It boomed when the railroad came and gas was discovered in Eastern Indiana in the late 1800s. Cars and semi trucks took business from the railroad and the natural gas ran out.

Redkey High School and its Redkey athletic teams were a source of pride for residents for decades. The Wolves basketball squads won sectionals in 1939 and 1952. Redkey High closed in the 1970s and a part of Redkey ceased to exist. Students now attend Jay County High in Portland, its athletes known as Patriots.

Gone, too, is Shambarger's Restaurant, which was famous for six decades, its seven-course meals of fine cuisine popular with diners from throughout the Midwest. Shambarger's closed in the 1980s. Four restaurants remain in town, but none are as well known outside Redkey.

One attraction, however, is gaining recognition across Indiana. It's the Key Palace Theatre at 123 South Meridian (Ind. 1). The old theater with 220 seats has been remodeled and expanded and now features blues and jazz music good enough to attract fans and put Redkey back on the map.

Owner Charlie Noble's Internet web site promises, "You can get up close and personal with entertainers" in the theater which is "keeping the blues alive." It is a place where "you can eat a Zeke's Monster Burger or go over to the other side and sit at a table."

"All this in little ol' Redkey," the promoter says, "in a place where fans are keeping the blues alive with friends."

"Little ol' Redkey," isn't so little as small towns go. Its 2000 census was 1,427, a gain of 44 over 1900. Ind. 1 enters town as Meridian Street past homes shaded with oak and locust trees.

Downtown, businesses remain amid the vacant store fronts of century-old buildings. Gold Medal Flour and Mail Pouch Tobacco signs cover the sides of a number of structures. A park is across from the police station and the 1905 city building.

It is summer and the Main Street Methodist Church reminds residents and visitors it is "Prayer Conditioned."

Redkey may not be the hot spot it once was, but it is worth a visit.

*　　*　　*

An IGA store is at the north edge of Redkey near where Ind. 1 crosses Ind. 67. In a lot off the road are the first horses we have seen since Dearborn County. An old church that has burned shows no indication it will be rebuilt. A round barn dated 1913 is at road side.

Ind. 1 crosses Ind. 26 six miles north of Redkey, then continues north three miles to Pennville.

PENNVILLE

Optimistic

If you're looking for someone in Pennville you'll likely find him or her sometime during the day at the Pennville Restaurant on Union Street (Ind. 1). It's a place for men to talk with men, women to chat with women and couples to meet with each other.

Many of the customers stop at the restaurant two or three times a day. If anything goes on in town, the locals can hear about it at the diner. A bulletin board is filled with notices of events around town.

Towns need spots like the Pennville Restaurant. After all, the American Legion Post down the street isn't open all the time, and postal inspectors sometimes frown if postmasters allow customers to engage in lengthy conversations.

The post office is up the street in the ground floor of the 1885 Masonic Hall. An auction house is in another section of the floor.

Pennville High School is now a part of Jay County High, but an elementary school remains on the northwest side.

Unlike many small towns, Pennville is growing, its 2000 population up by 69 to 706 over the last decade. More growth may come if the industrial park on the north side of town is developed.

*   *   *

A farm center is north of Pennville on Ind. 1. A mail box at one home is mounted on an old grindstone, once turned by the foot pedals that are still attached. A huge home, isolated from its less expensive neighbors, is under construction off the road.

Balbec, a pinpoint on the map, is less than two miles from Fiat, its neighbor to the north. Fiat isn't much bigger than an intersection with a beauty shop at one corner of Ind. 1 and Ind. 18. (See Ind. 18).

A mile to the north Jay County ends, and Wells County begins. A village called Nottingham is on Ind. 1. If there is a Robin Hood around or a Sherwood Forest in the area, neither is obvious.

PETROLEUM

Oil Is Well

Petroleum is another unincorporated tiny town on Ind. 1. It is seldom in the news, hasn't been since its school closed in 1966 and high school students sent to consolidated Southern Wells.

It was the Petroleum High Panthers that brought elation to fans over the years, winning high school sectional titles in 1913, when the team was among the final 16 teams, and again in 1946.

A post office remains. So does a garage, a knickknack shop and Robin's Nest antiques. What was once a grocery is closed.

For the curious on this day a prize antique car, an expensive model from an earlier era, is at road side. It is a jewel with a top that folds back, spare tires on the running boards.

Out front of an antique store are a washing machine with a wringer and a Coke machine, the kind in which soft drinks set in water cooled by ice. They are relics unseen by most Ind. 1 travelers too intent on their destination to enjoy the journey.

*   *   *

Farms continue to line each side of Ind. 1 between Petroleum and Reiffsburg, another crossroads town. A church is in the quiet community with well kept homes. A welding shop appears to be the only business in the town that's too small to have its own post office.

Farms are larger, the horizon wider on the six-mile drive into Bluffton, the Wells County seat.

BLUFFTON

Step into the "Parlor"

For downstate Hoosiers, Bluffton is one of Indiana's best kept secrets. It's on two lesser traveled roads, Ind. 1 and Ind. 124, and 15 miles from the nearest interstate.

Other than reports from patients who have visited the noted Bluffton Regional Medical Clinic, few southern Indiana residents hear much about the city. It is much more than a hospital town. It's a city of 9,536 with a historic—and attractive—downtown where most storefronts are occupied.

Bluffton is "Parlor City." Has been since the late 1800s. It's not just a prideful label. It's a distinction that still is deserved, town officials insist.

And it is one far different than the backwoods village that grew up on the Wabash after it was platted in 1838.

Legend says the "Parlor City" aphorism came from a visitor who noted streets had been paved with hard surface materials that were modern at the time. The pavement gave the city a neat appearance. The town's web site features a 1937 *Bluffton Evening-News Banner* story, which explains that "the parlor" once was the cleanest room and the one where guests were entertained.

The newspaper in unabashed boosterism added: "Bluffton still merits the reputation of being the most beautiful and well-kept city of the Hoosier state. It is picturesquely situated on the south bank of the far-famed Wabash River, crowning high bluffs from which it derives its name and which give it a commanding view of the surrounding country."

Wells County Courthouse

Pride in the city appears epidemic. Another web site notes, "We are about to make Bluffton a place you will have to visit at least once, just like Paris. No Eiffel Tower, but a fire tower at adjacent Ouabache (an Indian word for Wabash) State Forest. We have shopping, dining, sight-seeing, hiking and swimming, art shows and antiquing."

The River Greenway begins at Wabash River Park in the city, follows the Wabash for a time, then connects with trails within Ouabache State Park to form a five-mile walk.

A visitor notices right off that Bluffton is not your normal county seat town. The Wells County Courthouse is not on a square. It's at the corner of Main and Market, an impressive sandstone structure with a Romanesque design.

Market Street is shaded with trees and cars are angle parked. The 1898 Kapp block has three stories, alcoved windows and a castle-like top. Other buildings date back to 1892.

It is a downtown scene for many cities and towns with dilapidated buildings to envy.

Mayor Ted Ellis may be Bluffton's biggest booster. He notes: "Most people who have been to Bluffton were either visiting the Bluffton Regional Medical Center or our annual Street Fair. The Medical Center, whose roots lie in the Wells Community Hospital and the Caylor-Nickel Hospital, serves patients of the 60-plus physicians practicing in Bluffton. The Caylor-Nickel Research Foundation has been a pioneer in genetic research for decades.

"The Bluffton Free Street Fair, first held in 1898, is the oldest continuously-running street fair in the United States. Held the third week in September every year, it transforms the downtown into a giant party with rides, games, and food (which the doctors at the Medical Center advise us to avoid the other 51 weeks of the year!).

"Business owners here tell me the work ethic is strong and employee loyalty is high," the mayor adds.

Mayoral pride aside, visitors will be impressed when they step into the "Parlor" and are welcomed by this city on the river.

*   *   *

As Ind. 1 departs Bluffton to the north, it passes more fast food restaurants, a Wal-Mart center and the usual urban sprawl that now detracts from entrances and exits to small as well as large cities.

Five miles north of Bluffton, Ind. 1 crosses U.S. 224. A fireworks store is on the corner, the community of Kingsland just to the west.

"William Hunter," says a sign on a red barn in an area where homes begin to line the road as the road nears Fort Wayne and its suburbs.

OSSIAN

Home Town Convenience

It is soon apparent Ossian is a growing town, located as it is within a short drive to metropolitan Fort Wayne. A housing addition is at the south edge of the town, which grew in population from 2,428 to 2,943 from 1990 to 2000.

A business is at the south entrance to Ossian, where a billboard boasts that the Ossian State Bank is "locally owned and operated." Has been since 1912, the sign adds. Few towns, in this age of bank mergers, can make such a claim.

At least three churches, we observe, have day care centers. Churches have diversified; their responsibilities no longer Sunday only sermons.

This is a town that appears to be self-sufficient, its businesses varied. There are cafes, stores and shops, bakeries, a hardware and food stores.

High school students attend Norwell, a consolidation down on U.S. 224 to the south.

If there is a downside Ossian, it is not apparent. It is neat and clean, a nice place to come home to.

*   *   *

Ind. 1 has been repaved north of Ossian, a smooth drive commuters to jobs in Fort Wayne should appreciate. The terrain continues to be flat. Suburban homes separate the farms that remain.

Wells County ends and Allen County begins south of Yoder, a small community that grew up just west of Ind. 1 next to a railroad. A post office is in the unincorporated town.

Two miles from Yoder Road, Ind. 1 ends—for a distance—at Exit 116 on I-469, which arcs around Fort Wayne to the east. Ind. 1 resumes north of Fort Wayne and can be reached via either I-469 or I-69, which pass Fort Wayne to the west and north.

*   *   *

Indiana is a state of differing terrains and localities and these variations are observable as we travel Ind. 1 north from Fort Wayne.

Interstate Exit 116 leads off I-69 to Ind. 1 north of the Summit City. The road is narrow, more like a country lane than a state highway as its twists to the northeast. The speed limit is 50 mph and there are few opportunities for impatient drivers to exceed it. A few farms remain on the road as it winds its way to Leo-Cedarville.

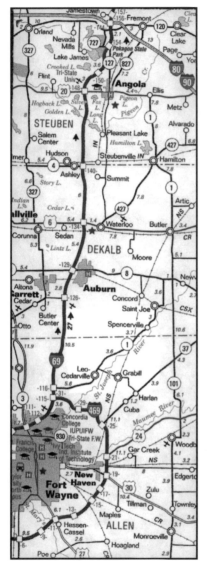

LEO-CEDARVILLE

One Plus One = One

Leo-Cedarville is a tale of two towns. It was formed within Cedar Creek Township in 1995 when Leo, population, 1,200 and Cedarville, population 570, agreed to merge. By 2000, the new municipality had 2,782 residents.

Both towns had their own histories. Cedarville, once a Potawatomi Indian village, is said to have been home for a time to Chief Metea, the noted orator for his people. Leo, platted in 1899, was named for Pope Leo XII.

The marriage of the towns seems to have been harmonious. Colorful Leo-Cedarville signs line the road that leads past a park, unobtrusive cafes, businesses and shops on Main Street at the river. All appear to blend in with the environment rather than detract from it.

Students attend Leo High School, youngsters play at nice parks and residents can attend services at the huge Mennonite Church or with other congregations.

It is an attractive community and residents may be more fortunate than they realize. Ind. 1 remains narrow as it follows the edges of Cedar Lake and the St. Joseph River. An improved highway could lead to rapid development which could ruin the serenity and the beauty of the drive.

*   *   *

Ind. 1 continues to follow the scenic St. Joseph, entering DeKalb County five miles north of what once was Leo. A cemetery is on each side of the twisting, tree-lined road as we near Spencerville.

SPENCERVILLE
Bridging the Years

A marker at St. Peter's Lutheran Church notes Spencerville was the site of the first white settlement in DeKalb County in 1828. The book, *Indiana: A New Historic Guide*, however, questions the claim, adding that the first land claim was not filed until 1833.

Reuben Dawson, the book reports, built a dam, sawmill and grist mill in 1836 and platted what is now Spencerville in 1842. The town's name is in honor of John Spencer, a clerk in the U.S. land office in Fort Wayne.

Much of the town, including the post office and the Eat'n Haus Restaurant, are on Main Street. Also in town are the Spencerville Community Club, the post office, a service center, a bank and a hair salon.

A covered bridge still crosses the St. Joseph near town, a 168-foot span upgraded in the 1980s.

Spencerville, unincorporated, depends on the DeKalb County sheriff's department for its police protection. Its high school closed in 1953 when students were sent to Riverdale at St. Joe. Students from both communities now attend Eastside High School in Butler.

*   *   *

From Spencerville, Ind. 1 curves through wet lands and farms where we see the first sheep we have noted on this drive.

ST. JOE
Town and Country

This is northeastern Indiana's lake country. A boat storage is off the road as we enter St. Joe, a nice residential community of 478 residents.

Country and town meet here at St. Joe Grain, St. Jude's restaurant, the bank and two churches. Town residents can meet at the two churches in town, debate issues at the Town Hall and attend parent-teachers meetings at Riverside Elementary.

Near town is Schekler's which boasts of its "fine pickles." A promotional sign is enough to make us try them.

It's a town worth more time than a casual visit.

*   *   *

North of St. Joe, the road turns east for a mile with Ind. 8 before turning back to the north. Butler is five miles ahead on Ind. 1.

BUTLER

A Northeastern Hub

Butler is 3.5 miles from the Ohio border but it's as Hoosier as most Indiana towns. It may, however, have more industry per person than most.

It has been a prime industrial location since the mid-1850s when the Lake Shore and Southern Railroad came through town. Another railroad followed and east-west U.S. 6 came later.

Butler, founded as Norristown in 1840, is today a city of 2,725 residents, many of whom work in factories around town.

Eastside High School, a consolidation of Butler and Riverdale, is in town. A popular stop for students and adults is the Broadway Café on Ind. 1 (South Broadway). A soda fountain in the restaurant serves cherry or vanilla phosphates, old-fashioned banana splits and other treats.

Butler may be out of the way in its northeastern Indiana location, but it is not out of place. It is worth a visit for anyone who is in the area.

*   *   *

"Artic," as the map notes, or "Arctic, as a sign at a railroad spells it, is a mile east of Ind. 1. Whatever! It's a hamlet of three homes, none of which are igloos.

Three miles north of the road to Artic (or Arctic), Ind. 1 ends its route due north and meanders to the northeast toward Hamilton where it crosses Ind. 427.

HAMILTON

By the Lake

Hamilton didn't just grow over the last decade, it mushroomed. The population increased 80 percent, from 685 in 1990 to 1,233 in 2000.

Hamilton Lake which extends to the north is Indiana's fifth largest. It attracts permanent residents and makes the town a summer destination for vacationers seeking water resorts. New houses are as common as older homes around the town that sits astride the DeKalb-Steuben County line.

Platted as Enterprise in 1836, it was soon renamed for Alexander Hamilton, whose life is portrayed on a mural near downtown. The business district can be reached on Wayne Street, which intersects with Ind. 1.

Hamilton retained its high school despite consolidation by absorbing some students from Metz, a rural school to the east.

A landmark on the nearby lake is the Cold Springs Hotel, which began as a resort on a farm in the late 1800s. A dance hall, added later, at times featured big bands. Few lake hotels are as old or as storied.

*   *   *

Ind. 1 continues north for eight miles where it ends its route at Ellis, which isn't much bigger than a crossroads.

*   *   *

It is a north-south route that reflects the variations of the state. We have not counted our stops, but there were at least 50. Each added to our appreciation of the state called Indiana and the people called Hoosiers.

INDIANA 3

Northeastern Indiana
Fort Wayne To Brighton

Contrasts mark Ind. 3 north from Fort Wayne. It is a typical four-lane route to U.S. 6, bypassing the small towns of Huntertown, LaOtto and Avilla. The terrain is level, the roads lined by farms and suburban expansion.

The road, heavily traveled, skirts the west edge of Kendallville, but an exit off the divided route leads into the town and its "Historic Main Street."

From Kendallville to Brighton, Ind. 3 is far different than to the south. It is a two-lane road through varied topography. Traffic is light, trucks are few. Lakes, small pockets created by nature, are numerous. The road rolls gently over terrain where cultivated fields are broken by woods and wetlands.

The drive is both tranquil and scenic.

KENDALLVILLE

It Makes, World Takes

Like most Hoosiers, we knew little about Kendallville, had visited the city only a couple of times earlier on brief stops. It exceeded our expectations.

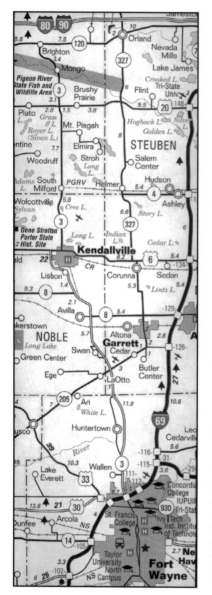

We stop again at Sharon's Breakfast House on South Main Street and find it remains a favorite place of residents to jump start their days. Cars and pickup trucks line the parking spaces as the sun rises over town.

Work crews share tables. Retirees swap stories. A few businessmen read the morning paper. A man, unshaven, his clothes tattered, sits on a stool at the counter reading a Bible as he sips coffee. Occasionally he stops to scribble notes.

One person is as valued as another for Sharon's is not a place for elitists.

"Downtown" is a few blocks up north. Chances are the "Historic Main Street" designation comes from the 19th century architecture in an area near the Mitchell Street intersection.

Stores offer a variety of merchandise. Many of the storefronts of old buildings are occupied in the city of 9,616 residents. It is Noble County's biggest—and only—city, and four times larger than Albion, the county seat. (See Ind. 9).

Industry is diverse, so much so the city has boasted "the world takes what Kendallville makes."

A golf course and park are on the west side of the city. On the east side is Bixler Lake, the site of a city park with swimming, fishing and camping areas.

*   *   *

On the west side of Ind. 3 is a 160-year-old mansion that is said to have been used as a stop on the "underground" railroad. The storied plantation-type landmark, built with brick, is fronted with four 25-feet high columns and topped with what appears to be a "widow's walk."

Original owner Stanley Whitford is said to have found gold in California, which financed construction of the mansion in 1844. If that is true, he must have kept quiet about his good fortune. It would be five years before another find set off the 1849 gold rush.

It is believed the home continued to be a station for slaves seeking freedom until Whitford sold the home in 1860. Its role in that pre-civil war era is marked by a sign along the highway.

Four miles north, homes are on the shores of Creek Lake. Noble County ends, and Lagrange County begins just south of the town of South Milford.

SOUTH MILFORD
No Fooling

South Milford isn't much bigger than a pen point on the map, but it has a grain company and a few businesses. Nearby are a hardwood company, a small steel fabricating plant and a boat storage business.

And it has a sense of humor. The "Two Fools" Bait and Tackle Shop is open to serve fishermen—and women—in search of big catches at area lakes. The post offices appears to be the center of the unincorporated community.

South Milford lost its high school in 1930, long before the consolidations of the 1960s. Students here now attend Prairie Heights.

*   *   *

Farms are small, their fields between lakes, but huge grain storage buildings dot the area. A sign designates a "River Friendly Farmer of Indiana."

Long Lake is to the east, Adams Lake to the west. A cemetery is on both sides of Ind. 3, south of the Maplewood Nature Center. A marker points to Lagrange County Park three miles to the west. Woodlands line the road for a short time before farms and silos that reach toward the sky reappear.

Ind. 2 crosses U.S. 20. A hamlet called Brushy Prairie is two miles to the east.

Traffic remains light as the road eases to the northwest through wooded lowlands. A Lion's Club sign offers a "Welcome to Mongo." Another marker indicates we are in the Pigeon River Fish and Wildlife Area.

MONGO

Beneath the Surface

Mongo, at first glance, doesn't appear to have much to offer a visitor. Its buildings are old, many in need of repair. Businesses are few. The tavern is closed until noon and not much else is open until then except the Mongo Country Store ("food, fishing and hunting supplies, beer and wine.)"

Mongo's beauty, however, is beneath the surface, much of it hidden in a more glorious past.

French fur traders bartered with the Potawatomi Indians, who called the outpost "Mongoquinong" for Big Squaw (or White Squaw) Prairie. Settlers soon shortened the name to Mongo.

It was here on Pigeon River where pioneers built a dam which formed a millrace to operate a grist mill and a distillery. Water power no longer is needed, but the millpond, now crossed by Ind. 3, remains. So does the dam, its overflow visible from a vantage point just to the west. Only the sound of the water, the songs of birds break the morning silence.

The millpond is not Mongo's only reminder of the past. The old two-story Mongo Hotel, a Victorian frame structure, is abandoned except for the clutter visible through its vertical windows.

What may be Mongo's oldest building stands, as it has since 1832, at the northeast corner of the town's main intersection. Across the corner is the tavern, which is in a 1916 brick building that was once a bank. Down the street across from the dam, is an 1876 two-story brick with a porch across the front.

Chances are it isn't the old structures that bring modern America to Mongo. It likely is its central location on Pigeon River and its 11,600 acres that are set aside for fish and wildlife. Blue-gill, bass, pike and trout are in its rivers and lakes. Deer, dove, upland game, squirrel and waterfowl can be hunted in season. Primitive camp sites and picnicking areas are open and canoeing is permitted.

Count Mongo as a hidden treasure on a road less traveled.

*   *   *

Ind. 3 curves to the northwest beyond the Mongo Methodist Church and passes vast farms with rich and productive soil. Irrigation equipment is in place on the vast flat fields should rains cease.

Off the road is English Prairie Church of the Brethren, a huge well-kept cemetery and Brighton Chapel Church.

BRIGHTON

With the Grain

Ind. 3 ends at Ind. 120 in Brighton, a town two miles from the Michigan border.

Except for homes, little remains in Brighton except its past. The old high school that was home to the "Wildcat" athletic teams, is now occupied by Christian Calvary Fellowship. Students from town have attended consolidated Lakeland High School since 1964.

Kauffman Farms with gigantic grain storage facilities across Ind. 120 from the school appears to be the biggest business in town. A garage is closed and there are no stores. Mail comes from the post office at Howe (see Ind. 9).

*   *   *

The drive has been easy, the scenery varied. The congestion of cities and the monotony of interstate travels have been forgotten. The pleasures await those who wish to make the journey from Kendallville north.

North To South
From Howe to Hope

Ind. 9 is a route that reflects a composite of Indiana. It passes through farms, skirts lakes, slows for small towns, bisects industrial cities and passes six historic courthouses and runs near two other seats of county government.

History unfolds along the road, labeled the "Highway of Vice Presidents" in tribute to three Hoosiers who served the nation in its second highest office.

Ind. 9 starts at the Michigan border where Mich. 66 runs north toward Sturgis. The Indiana Toll road parallels the state line. The town of Howe is a stone's throw to the south.

HOWE
Academically Inclined

Howe is no ordinary small town. It's home to 550 residents who live on shaded streets, congregate when they choose at the park in the center of town and dine amid conversation at the Town Square Restaurant.

A few blocks away is the coeducational Howe Military School for students from the fifth to twelfth grades. An average of 160 pupils attend classes on the imposing 100-acre campus with 15 buildings.

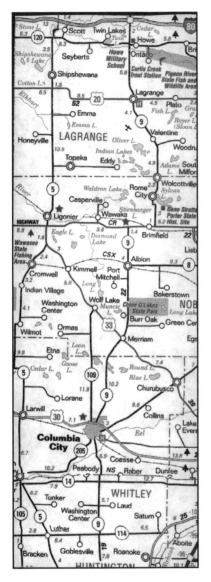

Students at Howe Military get special attention, the student-teacher ratio two-to-one for upper classes. High school subjects are many, varied and difficult, among them Latin, trigonometry, philosophy and military science. It is a curriculum exceeding that of today's high schools with enrollments that sometimes exceed 3,000.

Students who live in Howe attend Lakeland High School with an average enrollment of 700.

Howe's peaceful downtown is centered around the town square, which has a shelterhouse, benches, playground equipment and a basketball court. On the square is the Howe Market; the Kingsbury House, which began as a hotel in the 1860s and is now used for office space, the "Ice Cream is Happiness" store and the Town Square Restaurant.

The restaurant deserves more than a casual mention. We rated the Town Square as the best overall small town restaurant among 140 cafes we visited for our book *Main Street Diners - Where Hoosiers Start the Day.*

Owners Tom and Cindy Hackett take pride in "real" homemade foods, mashed potatoes, puddings, pie crust, dressing, bread and the huge cinnamon rolls, which are big enough to sate the appetite of the most famished customer.

The breakfast, lunch and dinner menus are varied, much more so than at most small town restaurants. The clientele is diverse. On a typical morning five or six men and women share a round table. Two women in their golden years are at a booth nearby. Couples of a younger age are at other tables. It is a harmonious group, one less boisterous than at cafes in towns where everyone seems to know each other.

Breakfast at the Town Square is a good place to start the day and a trip south on Ind. 9.

Back on the road, Ind. 9 crosses Ind. 120. Two service stations and the Howe Restaurant are at the intersection.

*   *   *

Just south of Ind. 120 we pass a horse drawn buggy, one of a number we will see in Lagrange County, which has the heaviest concentration of Amish and Mennonites in the state.

Off the road is a trailer park, a sharp contrast to the spacious old homes back in Howe. Ahead are halves of double wide homes being towed south from area plants where they are manufactured.

A farm offers brown eggs for sale, the color that some families prefer over white. The hue may mean something to buyers. Our "egg is an egg" mentality is unaware of any difference.

Urban sprawl is apparent even in farm country. Businesses have moved out along Ind. 9, which becomes Detroit Street as it enters Lagrange, the town.

LAGRANGE
Mural, Mural on the Wall

Most towns have more to offer than meets the eyes of a motorist who drives through on a state highway. Lagrange, a growing county seat town with 2,919 residents, is one of them. Much of its history can be observed on a stroll around the tree-shaded square.

A clock tower rises 125 feet above the dignified Renaissance Revival architecture that is reflected in the Lagrange County Courthouse, built of brick and accented with sandstone in 1879. On the lawn are the Friendship Gardens with ties to Grijpskerk, Lagrange's sister city in The Netherlands. A bandstand is in another area of the grounds. Enclosed disposal barrels, compliments of different organizations, help keep trash at a minimum.

Lagrange County Courthouse

The Town Hall and Carnegie Library are across the street from the square. Nearby is the First Presbyterian Church, another town landmark.

A mural covers the side of an old brick building at Detroit and Spring on the southeast corner of the square. The composite illustrates old scenes from around town, including a 1910 corn school, once an annual event, the old high school, churches and other reminders of an earlier time.

A Mexican grocery store on the square reflects the growing diversity of rural communities in northern Indiana. An art gallery, the Foltz Bakery, a Dollar Store, the Courthouse Café and the Courthouse Restaurant Lounge are among other businesses on the square. Law is a major enterprise in county seat towns and at least ten attorneys have offices across the streets from the Courthouse. Others are in adjoining blocks.

To the south along Ind. 9 are supermarkets, a hardware store and other commercial outlets.

At mid-morning, Mom's Restaurant at 404 South Detroit is crowded as usual with diners who appreciate the friendly atmosphere. It is a diner of choice for locals who come here to jump start their day with coffee and breakfast while exchanging friendly banter.

And it isn't at every restaurant a person can order "Mom's Skillet," which includes an egg topped with American fried potatoes, sausage gravy and cheese. A hungry person can't order that at McDonald's, which is just down the street.

Lagrange has moved out to the south as it has to the north on Ind. 9. The Sheriff's Department has relocated there as has the Lagrange County Publishing Company. A short distance away cars back up behind a horse drawn buggy, the road's shoulders too narrow for the driver to pull over.

*   *   *

An abandoned brick school once attended by elementary students indicates a more glorious past at the tiny community of Valentine, four miles south of Lagrange. What once was a playground is now a field of soybeans.

The Valentine United Methodist Church and the Zion Baptist Church remain among the 15 to 20 homes. A building that once housed a country store is vacant. Mckibben Farms, an agricultural operation, adjoins the community.

A housing boom will add to the town's population. Double-wide manufactured units as well as conventionally-built homes are being erected in a development at the south edge of Valentine.

The road continues to pass throughout farm country, the terrain slightly rolling, as it heads south toward Wolcottville. Some luxurious homes, one with a landscape yard on a lake site, are in the area. Five or six small natural lakes are along the five mile drive to Wolcottville.

WOLCOTTVILLE
One Town, Two Counties

Don't be surprised if one Wolcottville resident says he lives in Lagrange County while another insists he or she resides in Noble County. The town, population 933, straddles the border, although much of the business area appears to be in Lagrange County.

The county line isn't all that runs through Wolcottville. So do Ind. 9, which is Main Street, a railroad and Little Elkhart Creek.

Much of the business is on Main Street. The IGA market is there as is the post office, a Laundromat, an antique mall, a bank and other outlets. Off the street is the Wolcottville Grain Company. For a small town, Wolcottville offers enough conveniences to keep residents from making extra trips to larger cities to find much of what they need.

Area students who once were Wolcottville High Bulldogs now attend consolidated Lakeland High, home of the Lakers.

A stoplight on Ind. 9 marks the division of Lagrange and Noble Counties.

This is more than a one stoplight town. It is one worth a longer look than just a quick view from a car window at the 45 mile per hour speed limit.

*   *   *

An huge produce market is off Ind. 9 south of Wolcottville. Not far ahead is the Gaspar Catholic Church.

Way College, unfamiliar to us, is at Northport Road south of Wolcottville. A number of large structures are on the grounds, but a sign seems to discourage visitors. We learn later it is a college of Biblical Research. It was, prior to the mid-1970s, Kneipp Sanatorium, with accommodations for 200 guests. The Catholic Sisters of the Most Precious Blood once operated the sanatorium where the mineral water was believed to bring relief to patients with a variety of ailments.

ROME CITY
Scenery, History, Literature

For those who enjoy a lake setting, natural beauty and history, there is a lot to like about Rome City.

Welcome signs at the entrances to town note Rome City is "the home of Gene Strattan-Porter on beautiful Sylvan Lake."

Rome City itself is not much different from other communities. Ind. 9 divides much of the town of 1,615 residents from the lake to the east. In town are restaurants such as Stefano's Red Onion, Miller's Supermarket, a coin laundry, the fire and police departments, a medical center, a lounge or two and most of the services that help make it a self-sufficient resort area.

Attractive homes line much of the lake that hardly ripples in the calm of a peaceful summer day. Gene Strattan-Porter's home, a state historic site is almost hidden off the south edge of the lake. South from Rome City, the home is off Ind. 9 just over a mile to the east on County Road 900 North. Branches of trees stretch

Gene Strattan-Porter home

from each side over the narrow lane, forming a tunnel toward the home.

The setting at dawn seems as remote and as tranquil as it may have been when the author-naturalist chose it almost a century ago. Only the noise of birds is heard amid the towering trees. The grounds and gardens can be seen at a visitor's leisure and questions about the habitat may be answered by an on-site naturalist. Tours of the home, called "The Cabin in the Wildflower Woods," are available on the hour from 9 a.m. to 4 p.m. Tuesday through Saturdays and from 1 to 4 p.m. on Sundays.

Windows from the second floor gave Strattan-Porter a great view of the lake. It was, no doubt, an inspiration for some of her twelve novels and her nature poems and essays.

Memo to women: If your husbands prefer golf to history, drop them off at the Limberlost Golf Course between Ind. 9 and the entrance to the Gene Strattan-Porter site. They can enjoy their game while you browse around the grounds and spend a few dollars at the gift center.

*   *   *

Three miles south of Rome City, Ind. 9 merges with U.S. 6 and goes west into the town of Brimfield. Not much remains in

Brimfield except an expansive lumber company and a few houses. The post office no longer is open in the unincorporated hamlet.

Ind. 9 turns south a mile to the west and resumes its route down the state. Albion, the Noble County seat, is four miles ahead.

ALBION

Freedom from Clamor

It is soon obvious Albion is a neat town where residents care about their property. A woman sprays her manicured lawn. Down the street, another homeowner sweeps the walks around his home.

Downtown, if a town of 2,284 can have a downtown, is slow to awaken. The Noble County Courthouse is open but few residents are seeking the services of officials. A law office clerk arrives with documents to be processed.

The Noble County seat was moved to Albion in 1846 after brief locations in Augusta and Port Mitchell. Two courthouses occupied the Albion square before the current Richardsonian Romanesque structure was built in 1889. It is imposing, castle-like, with rounded corners, brick accented with limestone, a clock in the tower. A gazebo is on the ground.

To the west is the old Noble County Jail, called "an eclectic mix of Gothic and Second Empire styles." Bars remain on the cells in the prison area. The only "inmates" now are those who incar-

Noble County Courthouse

cerate themselves in order to peruse documents kept by the Noble County Historical Society. The Historic Landmarks Foundation helped fund a restoration plan for the structure.

Businesses and law offices are in buildings erected after the railroad brought prosperity to the town in the late 1800s. On the square, too, is "Doc's Hardware," which dates back to an earlier era. It is a welcome stop for anyone unimpressed with the giant Lowe's and Menards of today.

Central Noble High School, a consolidation of Albion and Wolf Lake, is on Cougar Court in Albion.

Anyone who wants a respite from the noise, clamor and pollution of big city life will enjoy a stop in Albion. Restaurants are few and the Dairy Queen, one of the few franchises in town, doesn't open for breakfast.

*   *   *

South of Albion, a good place to stop for breakfast—or for lunch—is the Half Acre Café, which is bright, clean and recently remodeled.

It is obvious from the name and the appearance that this is a restaurant that caters to farm folks. Two old Allis-Chalmers tractors, one hitched to a moldboard plow, are parked facing Ind. 9 at the north and south entrances onto the crushed stone parking area.

Inside, the walls are lined with pictures of rural scenes and relics once used by farmers. The floor is tile, the tables look new, the place appears neat and clean—and the food is good.

Place mats on this June day include a schedule of the Noble County Community Fair in July.

For back home cooking, stop at the Half Acre. You'll be as pleased as a farmer will be with a bumper crop.

Houses are being built on a small lake across Ind. 9 from the Half Acre.

CHAIN O'LAKES

One Park, Eight Lakes

Further evidence we are in lake country is the Chain O'Lakes State Park east of Ind. 9. It is the closest place to heaven a boater will find. It is possible to paddle through eight connecting lakes or hike trails in a setting far removed from the bluster of modern life. A nature center in an old school is an ideal stop for families with children.

The park, with a swimming beach and picnic locations, is a place to fish, camp and enjoy cross-country skiing.

It is suggested that families combine a stop at Chain O'Lakes with a visit to the Gene Strattan-Porter home.

*   *   *

Burr Oak, not far south of the park entrance, is a community not much bigger than the pen point on the Indiana map. Not much remains except the Burr Oak Baptist Church.

Farms and woodlands cover the terrain toward Merriam, a crossroads town where Ind. 9 crosses U.S. 33. What once was the District No. 4 School (built in 1914) is now privately owned.

The Cornerstone Wesleyan Church and the Merriam Christian Chapel are in the unincorporated crossroads community. So are a garage, a convenience store and a few small industries.

Noble County ends, Whitely County begins south of Merriam. More lakes are off Ind. 9 to the west, and Tri-County Park is in the area. Lots are for sale at Magic Hills Estates near the Magic Hills Golf Course.

En route into Columbia City are the St. Matthew's United Methodist Church, which calls attention to its two ice cream socials in this summer of 2001, and the Thorncreek Church of God.

A sprawling apartment complex is to the east of Ind. 9. Four-lane U.S. 30 is just ahead, making the rental units easily accessible for tenants to jobs in Fort Wayne (15 miles to the east). Not far from the apartments are stables for the Fort Wayne Horse Patrol.

COLUMBIA CITY
Cigars and Coneys

Much of U.S. 30 through the north edge of Columbia City is lined with strip malls and commercial enterprises. As in other cities, downtown no longer is the destination of choice for shoppers who prefer to park in spacious lots and avoid long walks to stores.

A Dairy Queen, much larger than most, is south of the intersection on Ind. 9 which enters Columbia City as Main Street. It is a growing city, its 2000 population 7,077, up 1,371 over the previous decade.

Businesses disappear a short distance from U.S. 30 and Main Street passes through a residential area. Flags fly in front of old, well-kept homes with neat lawns, a sharp contrast to the commercial area to the north.

Whitley County Courthouse

Columbia City's centerpiece is the majestic Whitley County Courthouse, its white sandstone glistening in the sun. Its Renaissance design features rounded corners, dormer-type windows and a clock tower topped with a dome. Opened in 1890, it is one of the state's most impressive courthouses.

Whitley County was formed in 1838 and named for Col. William Whitley, an Indian fighter, soldier and pioneer killed in battle. The city's most famous son, however, is Thomas Riley Marshall, who became Indiana governor (1909-1913) and U.S. vice president (1913-1921). It was Marshall who said, "What the country needs is a really good five-cent cigar." A sentence like that 75-years later would bring a reprimand from anti-smokers and health officials.

Marshall's office was across the street at the corner of Van Buren and Chauncey in an 1888 building that also housed a dry goods store. Some of the city's notable homes are to the north on Chauncey Street. Many of its oldest commercial buildings, circa 1889-1893, remain on Van Buren, a shopping area that extends to the west from the courthouse.

Many of the store fronts are occupied; a few are vacant. Most are closed, however, on this day for the annual Old Settlers Days. "Will reopen next week," read signs on some windows. Van Buren is closed to traffic, the street crowded with Poor Jack's carnival rides, games and food booths.

Among restaurants open is The Nook, "home of the original Coney Island." The aroma is enticing, the prices reasonable, an old-fashioned fish sandwich $1.75. It's an institution, a household name more familiar to some area residents than Thomas Marshall.

Marshall's home on West Jefferson Street is now the Whitley County Historical Society Museum.

If you like history, architecture, stylish courthouses or "original" coneys, Columbia City is a good place to spend some time.

*   *   *

Huntington is 19 miles to the south, Marion 40 miles. Few towns are along the route. The Country Post Inn—"surf and turf - $11.95"—at the south edge of Columbia City is one of a few places to dine on the drive.

Five miles to the south, Ind. 9 crosses Ind. 14. The Crossroads Inn Restaurant and a heavy equipment business are at the intersection. So is an old corner school, now restored as a residence.

Farms have been small and the terrain has undulated south from the Michigan border. The lake country is now back to the north. The land now flattens, the fields grow larger, the horizon becomes more expansive. It is the ever-changing landscape that helps make Indiana a state of contrasts.

A short distance to the south, five silos tower over the topography to the east near a community marked Laud on our map. Our curiosity takes us over a county road that leads to the community of a few homes and what looks like an old general store.

The silos to the south, we learn, are at a farm called Bittersweet Acres, a giant diary operation with a number of barns and other structures. The buildings are neat and clean. It is there that Prairie Farms milk, often seen at supermarkets, is produced.

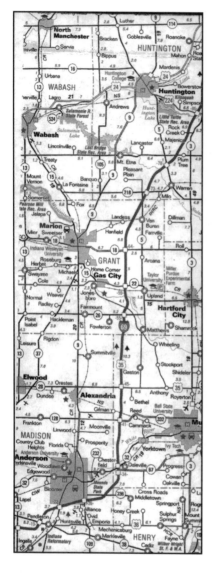

Back on Ind. 9 the road crosses Ind. 114, which separates Whitley County from Huntington County.

Farms abut the road as it continues south toward Huntington. A white barn is lettered "Good Earth" in gratitude for the rich soil.

Ind. 9 joins four-lane U.S. 24 as it bypasses Huntington to the north and east. Off the road are the Huntington College campus, with 700 students, and Huntington North High School, with 2,100 pupils from throughout the city and the rest of Huntington County. The college moved to Huntington from Hartsville in 1897. (See Ind. 46 chapter). Ind. 9 continues south as a four-lane road when U.S. 24 resumes its route to the west.

HUNTINGTON
Museum City

Motorists who skirt the city of Huntington will miss its historic downtown and its Indian, river and railroad heritages. We choose to enter Huntington from the west on Park Street, which proves to be a good choice.

Overlooking the street is the Spanish-style Victory Noll Convent, home of Our Lady of Victory Missionary Sisters. Not far ahead is the St. Felix Friary, circa 1928, a European-style brick-walled manor which is now a Church of the Brethren parish.

Nearer downtown on Park Street is Memorial Park and its sunken gardens in what once was a limestone quarry. The gardens, with two stone pedestrian bridges, have been an attraction since 1929.

Huntington County Courthouse

Huntington's past, however, extends far beyond the 1920s. Miami Indians, who established a village on the banks of the Wabash, called their settlement Wepecheange. White settlers began moving into the area in the early 1830s and renamed the town for Samuel Huntington, a signer of the Declaration of Independence.

The settlement grew slowly, then boomed when the Wabash and Erie Canal opened. Canal usage declined when railroads came and Huntington became a train town.

The canal is gone. U.S. 24 and Ind. 9 bypassed Huntington. The railroad remains, however. Trains rumble through the heart of the city, their whistles echoing off walls of buildings as old as the tracks. And Huntington continues to grow. Its population of 17,450 reflected a 6.5 percent increase from 1990.

Near the railroad is the 1906 Huntington County Courthouse, built of stone, Neoclassical in design, its four stories topped by a dome. Murals in the courthouse interior illustrate the area's early history. The Huntington County Historical Society is on the fourth floor.

It is not the only museum in the city that focuses on history.

The Dan Quayle Center and Museum not far from the Courthouse contains an exhibit of Quayle's 1989-1993 vice presidency. Quayle, who served in both the U.S. House and the U.S. Senate, grew up in Huntington and attended school in the city where his family published the *Huntington Herald* daily newspaper.

The Wings of Freedom Museum displays aircraft, artwork, historic documents and aircraft that includes a restored P-51 Mustang. Elsewhere in the city, the Fords of the Wabash Park help illustrates the era before the Indian culture was replaced by that of white settlers.

Huntington's history also is depicted in a sesquicentennial museum on the side of a downtown building. It portrays the "Historic Community in Action" for 150 years.

Cities though are about people. It is a warm afternoon and Ed Fugate is eager to talk to visitors. He's seated on a bench out front of what was the fashionable LaFontaine Hotel in an era before roads bypassed cities and motels attracted travelers.

Fugate lives in the old hotel, now known as LaFontaine Center which houses senior citizens and the disabled. "I love it," he says of his home here. "It's quiet (except for the trains). I can walk to stores, and I come and go as I choose. My studio apartment has a kitchen, so I can either cook my meals or come downstairs and eat. It's really a nice place."

Everyone should be as happy in this era of criticism and constant complaints.

*   *   *

Back on the road, Ind. 9 crosses the Wabash and continues its four-lane divided route south. It is a road less personal and void of the character that makes travelers feel they are a part of their surroundings. It's like driving on an interstate, the miles passing by with little attention to what exists beyond the pavement.

It is that way as Ind. 9 angles to the southwest from Huntington. Eight miles to the south, the road crosses the eastern tips of state-operated Salamonie Lake, a year-around facility where visitors can fish, boat, hike, snowmobile or camp.

Ind. 9 crosses Ind. 114 south of the lake. Just to the east from the intersection is Mt. Etna.

MT. ETNA
It's So Small . . .

Mt. Etna is so small its town offices are at 5930 South 588 West. That's a Huntington address. Mt. Etna isn't big enough to have a post office.

"Indiana's smallest town," a sign on Ind. 114 boasts. It's a nice motto, but it isn't true. The population in 2000 was 110, a loss of one over the 1990 total.

Other, towns, though, are smaller. Mt. Etna would need to lose 109 residents to match the one person a census taker found down in New Amsterdam, an Ohio River town that isn't much bigger than a canoe. And Mt. Etna still has 81 more people than Laconia in Harrison County.

The Internet reveals Mt. Etna has a town government and a bait shop, but not much more. Actually, it is big enough to straddle Ind. 124, have a few houses and a nice church. And four-lane Ind. 9 is nearby for quick trips to Huntington to buy postage stamps, groceries and whatever can't be bought at the bait and tackle shop.

Oh, there are some other things Mt. Etna doesn't have. There are no traffic jams, air pollution, noise, suburban sprawl or bright lights that dim the evening stars.

*   *   *

Ind. 9 narrows to two lanes from a four-lane divided route midway between Ind. 124 and Ind. 218 and continues through prime farm land toward Marion.

MARION
Clutter on the Bypass

Ind. 9 again becomes a four-lane route as it enters the northeast side of Marion and merges for a time with Ind. 15. The roads are lined with the usual congestion of businesses, including those at the North Park shopping center.

Shopping complexes are a paradox; convenient for shoppers, clutter for the environment. They are that way in Marion, population 31,320, as they are elsewhere. They often leave false impressions with motorists who do not leave the bypasses to see what is in the heart of those cities.

(See Marion in Ind. 18 chapter).

Ind. 9 joins Ind. 37, a wide expanse of concrete designed to handle heavy traffic through the commercialized west side of Marion. The road splits from Ind. 37 to the south, narrows to two lanes and enters a residential area.

*   *   *

An airport is off to the west near the intersection with Ind. 22, which leads east to Jonesboro and Gas City. We have returned to farm country, the fields flat, the farms large. Ind. 9 crosses Ind. 26 a mile east of Fairmount.

(See Fairmount in Ind. 26 chapter).

Ind. 9 continues its route due south, passing Madison-Grant High School, "home of the Argylls" and a consolidation of Fairmount and Summitville. The Madison-Grant name is appropriate, the school near the border that separates Grant from Madison County. As are many consolidated schools, Madison-Grant is in a rural setting, away from the distractions of towns and traffic.

This is prime farm country, but homes on small acreage are along the road, rural havens for families who prefer elbow room to small lots in towns.

To the south a road leads a mile east to Summitville.

SUMMITVILLE
Off The Beaten Path

At first glance a visitor might think Summitville is lost in time. No state highway leads into town. A high school no longer gives the town recognition. A Madison County web site barely give it space on the Internet. And it's not on the mainstream of Indiana tourism, now that passenger trains no longer run through town on the railroad. Only the curious detour off Ind. 9 to observe what is here.

None of those things stopped the town from growing in the last decade. Its 2000 population was 1,090, up 80 from 1990.

A bank remains, so do the Corner Market, a flower shop and other small businesses that are clustered in the area around Main and Mill Streets. Buildings in the center of town date beyond 1895, including one that is a flat iron structure from that era.

Doctors offices, a library, an elementary school and a community library are within walking distance for most residents. And walking is easy for there is little traffic at mid-day. On a residential street, two tykes ride bikes, a woman guides a riderless bicycle, a second pushes a buggy and two toddlers stroll beside them. They occupy much of the pavement, knowing they are safe from speeding cars.

Police and firemen are available in case of emergencies.

Summitville may have seen more prosperous times, but most folks here think it still is a good place to call home.

*   *   *

Out on Ind. 9, the road continues south to Alexandria.

ALEXANDRIA
"Democracy in Action"

"Small Town USA." signs greet visitors to Alexandria. More about that later.

Alexandria was created to be a canal town. The canal never arrived but two railroads, an interurban, Ind. 9 and Ind. 28 did. So did a the gas boom of the 1880s, a company that made the

Aladdin and other lamps, and entrepreneurs who pioneered the rock wool industry.

Town founders gambled on the site being on the route of the proposed Center Canal. They lost. The canal boom faded and so did hopes for the water route. Gas brought the usual glass factories and brickyards and increased the population tenfold to more than 7,000 in the decade prior to 1900.

Scene in downtown Alexandria

Gas supplies dwindled as they did elsewhere in east central Indiana. Other industries helped offset the loss, but the population declined for much of the 20th Century. That trend has changed. The 2000 census showed the city had 6,260 residents, a gain of 551 over the last decade.

Indiana's first interurban began its runs between Alexandria and nearby Anderson on Jan. 1, 1898. It also was said to be the first electric railroad designed for city-to-city service. A marker at the terminal site—now a small park at Harrison and Church—claims the interurban made the area the traction center of the United States.

Commuters caught in traffic jams today can only dream of expedient travel on interurban lines.

Ind. 9 bypasses (to the east) the downtown area, leaving Harrison Street as the main route through the heart of the city. Canal Street, a reminder of the hopes of its founders, runs parallel to Harrison. Some of the three-story buildings are as ancient as the gas boom.

That "Small Town USA" designation came in WWII when an Office of War Information cited it in a booklet as an example of democracy in action. The pamphlet was reproduced in 1976 when America observed its bicentennial.

Most Hoosiers today know "Alex" (as locals know the city) for the Alexandria High School basketball teams, which year in, year out, are among the best in their classification.

Ind. 9 skirts the southeast edge of town where traffic is delayed by a freight train. Along the route is the city park and swimming pool, crowded on a hot summer day with youngsters more interested in the joy of the moment than Alexandria's past.

*   *   *

To the south, Ind. 9, once a rural drive, no longer is a road less traveled. It has approached the city of Anderson. The road becomes four lane near the T-intersection with Ind. 128. Linwood is off to the west, a community called Prosperity off to the east.

At the north edge of Anderson, Ind. 9 cuts to the southeast and becomes Satterfield Road, a major thoroughfare. Off the street are Mounds Mall, a shopping center; Hoosier Park, a harness track; and Anderson College. Restaurants are numerous—25 at least—before the road reaches a busy interchange with I-69.

Anderson is an industrial city of 60,000 residents and the Madison County seat of government. A number of historic sites and points of interest are in a downtown area bounded by 8th and 12th and Central and Delaware.

*   *   *

Ind. 9 accompanies I-69 west to the first interchange where it resumes its route to the south, passing through unincorporated Huntsville before skirting Pendleton.

Madison County ends, Hancock County begins. Farms again abut the road. Eden, another hamlet without a town government, is just to the south. Eden may not be paradise, but it's a quiet community that still recalls the celebrations that followed the back-to-back Eden High School basketball championships of 1945 and 1946.

Eden students now attend Greenfield Central with one-time rivals Maxwell and Greenfield.

Maxwell, to the south on Ind. 9, remains unincorporated, but new homes appear on what once was farm land. Grain silos appear as backdrops to housing developments and it is difficult to tell whether the area is an extension of Indianapolis to the east or of Greenfield to the north.

GREENFIELD
Riley's Town

Greenfield has sprawled north to the I-70 interchange and beyond turning the entrance into Fast Food Boulevard. Each side of Ind. 9 from the interstate into town is occupied with restaurants, businesses and other developments.

Greenfield no longer is the small, dreamy town James Whitcomb Riley knew.

It is now a city of 14,600 residents, a 25 percent increase in population from 1990 to 2000. Traffic snarls are common on Ind. 9 and a new bypass has been suggested. Life for residents no longer is the same.

Ind. 9 crosses U.S. 40, the old National Road, an east-west route on the north side of the Hancock County Courthouse. Despite the changes around it, the Courthouse remains much as it has since it opened in 1896. Built of limestone and accented with a red roof, it has rounded corners on an impressive clock tower that can be seen for miles across the flat terrain.

The old jail is across from the Courthouse.

Hancock Courthouse (left), old jail (right)

A statue of Riley, the Hoosier Poet, is on the north side of the Courthouse. His home is a few hundred feet west on Main Street (U.S. 40). The Riley Memorial Park, bisected by Brandywine Creek, is east on Main.

Ind. 9 continues south as it exits Greenfield past a small strip mall. A soybean field is almost hidden by houses that continue to line the road. New homes adjoin fields, leaving suburbanites and farmers to peacefully co-exist.

Hancock County ends, Shelby County starts six miles to the south. Ind. 9 crosses U.S. 52 just east of Fountaintown. The Brandywine Creek valley parallels the road toward Shelbyville. The land is fertile, the crops productive.

SHELBYVILLE
Another Vice President

It is soon obvious Shelbyville no longer is immune from suburban growth, even though it is 27 miles to the heart of Indianapolis. Apartment units cover the northwest section of the I-74-Ind. 9 interchange. A golf course is across Ind. 9 to the east. It is two miles to downtown, a route marked with restaurants, motels and convenience stores.

It is no surprise the city's population grew by 17 percent to 17,951 from 1990 to 2000.

Ind. 9 meanders into downtown Shelbyville and becomes Harrison Street. It was on Harrison Street where Thomas Hendricks lived before moving to Indianapolis and later becoming the nation's Vice President under Grover Cleveland in 1885.

To the south is the Public Square, site of a bronze statue that reflects attorney-lawyer Charles Major's novel *Bears of Blue River*, which has its setting in Shelby County.

The Public Square is not to be confused with the County Courthouse, one of the state's newest (1936). The Courthouse, a stone building more modern than architecturally significant, faces Ind. 9. It is one of the few in Indiana not on a square.

*   *   *

Ind. 9 exits Shelbyville through a residential area void of unsightly commercial enterprises. It is 16 miles to Hope, the only sizable town to the south on the road.

Farms begin at the outskirts of Shelbyville and the road is again less traveled. A combine lumbers on the pavement, not a detraction to the driver of a single car that waits to pass.

The terrain is level, the road straight. A church off the highway appears to have once been a school.

Wilson is a hamlet at the edge of the road. The Lewis Creek Baptist Church and cemetery are at the crossroads where Country Crafts Corner appears to be the only business.

What looks to be a pioneer cemetery is a short distance south of Wilson. A rural road leads southeast toward Geneva, a small town on the Flatrock River crossed by Ind. 9. The terrain, which has been flat, becomes rolling in the area.

Norristown, another small community, is just east of Ind. 9. Twenty or so homes, the Farmers Masonic Lodge and the Norristown Community Church are in the town on Shelby County Road 1100 South. A huge cemetery fronts onto Ind. 9.

Shelby County blends into Bartholomew County just south of Norristown. Farmsteads are near the road, one whose barn is only 20 feet from the pavement.

A jokester has added a "Hee" in front of a sign for "Haw" Creek not far from where the speed limits drops to 35 mph at the north entrance to Hope.

HOPE

Surprise! Surprise!

"A Surprising Little Town," boasts a sign at the entrance to Hope. It is indeed surprising, so much so we called it a "Golden Nugget" in our book, *Backroads Indiana.*

It has more to offer than is expected for town of 2,140 residents. Two museums are in the heart of Hope, which has a bank, a number of stores, a library and a town square.

The Yellow Trail Museum contains artifacts of historical significance. The term "Yellow Trail," according to *Indiana: A New Historic Guide,* originated when a filling-station owner marked telephone poles with yellow paint, creating a trail which led to his business. The Yellow Trail, in a narrow two-story building at the southwest corner of Main and Jackson, contains various items from the past. It is not always open, but drums, phonographs, radios, toys, pictures and other antiques can be seen through the large windows.

Across the street in the tree-shaded park is the Indiana Rural Letter Carriers Museum. It's an appropriate location for the first rural free delivery started from Hope in 1896. The small frame museum has items used by post offices and rural carriers who delivered the mail with horses and buggies. It is said to be the only museum of its kind in the nation.

A shelterhouse, bandstand, benches and playground equipment also are in the square where a marker notes that a Moravian Church held the first services in Hope in 1830. (A Moravian Church is now at the south edge of town on Ind. 9).

A youth center on the north side of the square is open to youths 6 to 19 from 6 to 11 p.m. Fridays and Saturdays.

The Filling Station Restaurant, where cars once were serviced, offers fine food at its location on the south side of the square. The Sweetie Pie nearby dispenses bakery items.

This is a town with a Chamber of Commerce and a sense of community that is proof small towns can survive in eras of change.

                              *   *   *

Hauser High School, a consolidation of Clifford and Hope, is off Ind. 9 at the south edge of town. Cars fill the parking lot, an indication many of the students from rural areas drive—rather than ride buses—to classes.

A housing addition is near the school where the average attendance is 300 in the four grades.

Farms again appear. The road passes a sign to a winery, crosses Clifty Creek and ends six miles south of Hope at Ind. 46. (Ind. 9 once continued south, then east before ending at Ind. 7. That section is now designated as Ind. 46).

                              *   *   *

Ind. 9 is a cross-section of the state. It is rural, it is urban. It is farms, it is cities and towns. It passes through an era where four vice presidents had their start. It is home to the literature of Gene Strattan-Porter and Charles Major and the poetry of James Whitcomb Riley. It is Indiana.

INDIANA 135

Indianapolis To Mauckport
Road Of Contrasts

Ind. 135 is urban and rural. It is flat, it is hilly. It is straight, it is winding. It passes rich farms to the north, fields between ridges to the south. It is heavily traveled to the north, Less traveled to the south. It is a 149-mile drive much like Indiana, a composite of variations.

*　　*　　*

The road begins on Indianapolis' south side and remains congested as it heads south toward the Johnson County border.

Businesses blanket each side of four-lane Ind. 135 from the county line to beyond Smith Valley Road. The commercial sprawl continues to devour farms and fields.

Commuters who moved to the area to escape the city now live among the commercialism of the suburbs. The road is their congested drive to work. It is their escape route home.

Ind. 135 narrows to two lanes, but traffic remains heavy on the route. It will remain heavily traveled until it reaches Nashville.

New homes extend past the once rural communities of Stone's Crossing and Bargersville. The expansion has reached Trafalgar, another Johnson County town 22 miles from Indianapolis. More homes are under construction and new businesses are opening.

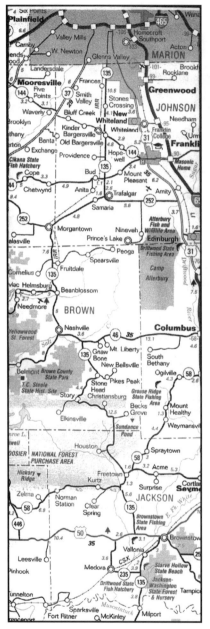

Once a quiet farm town, Trafalgar recorded a 50 percent increase in population—from 521 to 798—in the decade before 2000.

Ind. 135 joins Ind. 252 at the south edge of Trafalgar where the road runs southwest, passes the community of Samaria and continues to Morgantown, crossing from Johnson to Morgan County.

Urban growth has yet to reach Morgantown, a "gateway" to Brown County.

Businesses, antique shops and restaurants often are stops for sightseers en route to Nashville and Brown County. Kathy's, a popular restaurant that features home cooking and excellent pies, is usually crowded with travelers and local residents.

Ind. 135 leaves Ind. 252 in the heart of Morgantown, population 964, and resumes its route south. Morgan County ends, Brown County begins two miles to the south. Farm lands fade into the hills of Brown County.

The road passes through the communities of Fruitdale, then Beanblossom. To the south the road rises onto a ridge where a vista opens onto a view of Beanblossom to the north and hills to the west.

Ind. 135 then follows a ridge south into Nashville.

NASHVILLE
Escape the Routine

Ask Hoosiers to cite an Indiana county at random and chances are they will name Brown. It may be the state's best known county, not because of its industry, its farms, its schools or its athletes, but because of its natural attractions.

Up to four million visitors a year come to Nashville, a Gatlinburg of the north, and other areas of the county to view its wondrous beauty and the display of colors nature paints on the wooded hills each autumn.

Less than a third of the land in the county is farmed, the rest is woods and hills, choice sites, scenic and remote, for those who seek to escape cities and subdivisions.

Residents are far different than they were when Ernie Pyle described them back in 1940, a few years before he lost his life while a war correspondent.

Pyle wrote: "The typical Brown County man plays a guitar in the woods, and raises a little tobacco; and goes to church, and drinks whiskey, and is a dead shot with a squirrel gun. And there are even those who can kill a squirrel with a rock as easily as with a gun."

Brown County residents today are more cosmopolitan—businessmen, career women, retired professionals, shopkeepers, lawyers and salesmen, who may drive daily to offices in Bloomington, Columbus or Indianapolis.

Telling others about Nashville is like lecturing ministers on the Bible. Most readers likely know as much about the town as we do even after one hundred or more visits.

It bills itself as a "Pioneer Art Colony." It is that and more. It's an attraction for tourists be they interested in art salons, food, overnight lodging, gifts or a return to the quaintness of a small town that keeps the past alive by catering to 21st Century tastes.

Those who may call it a glorified tourist trap are blind to the ambiance that surrounds them as they stroll through the narrow streets and squeeze into crowded shops. It is a place to reflect on a time when Kin Hubbard's rustic Abe Martin espoused Brown County's cracker barrel philosophy in 300 newspapers.

Sure! A parking spot may be hard to find, streets may be difficult to cross and sidewalks may be packed. Those things are part of Nashville's fascination.

To be in Nashville is to be among a crowd in search of an experience different from cities and towns where the next stop is like the one ahead. Nashville is variety, a respite from the usual.

It is a place to watch stage shows, shop at an old country store, dine in a restaurant that began as a general store 130 years ago or spend an afternoon at an art gallery or a historical museum.

And to visit the pastoral Brown County Courthouse, which appears little changed over 13 decades. If tired, find a liars' bench on the Courthouse lawn. A character as quaint as Abe Martin may sit down beside you and reveal his own brand of humor.

*   *   *

At the south edge or Nashville, Ind. 135 joins Ind. 46 to the east for three miles, passing motels, a shopping complex and the east entrance to Brown County State Park, Indiana's largest state park.

Three miles from Nashville Ind. 135 turns south off Ind. 46 and begins its wandering route toward Freetown. It has become a road less traveled. It twists through a community called Camp Roberts where houses are located between the pavement and a small creek.

The valley ends, the hills begin, as the road skirts the eastern edge of Brown County State Park. To the south it enters Pleasant Valley and passes Van Buren Elementary School. A high school by that named ceased to exist in 1958 and students from the area now attend Brown County High in Nashville.

A short distance south, Ind. 135 makes a 90-degree turn west where New Bellsville Pike runs east. In a front yard to the south is the famed Stone Head marker, the head of a man carved into a five-foot high slab of sandstone.

Henry Cross, a farmer who sometimes engraved tombstones, is said to have created the marker in 1851 rather than work out his tax payment on roads.

PIKE'S PEAK
Generally Speaking

A detour off Ind. 135 is recommended. About 1.5 miles east on New Bellsville Pike is the community of Pike's Peak, named, it is said, when a covered wagon headed west to Pike's Peak, Colorado, broke down. The passengers, undeterred, ended their journey and named the place after their original destination.

Pike's Peak's biggest attraction is Crouch's Market, a general store, restaurant, museum, picture gallery and recreation center worth a stop. It's a place to have signatures witnessed by a notary public, to buy firewood, to learn the latest news, and to relax.

Inside are items that make Crouch's a general store: Hardware, plumbing supplies, garden tools, nails, stove pipes, nuts and bolts, caps, gloves, milk, groceries, assorted meats and ice cream.

Sandwiches and snacks are available, so are tables for diners in a rear section that doubles as a museum. Pictures of hunters with their deer and wild turkey are on a wall. So are snapshots of fishermen with their catches.

On an opposite wall is a history of the town with a story of how Pike's Peak got its name. News clippings and pictures add to the lore of the community. An old penny scale weighs visitors and forecasts their fortunes. An ancient foot-pedaled grindstone is in the store where a part of America's past remains.

*   *   *

Back on Ind. 135, the road runs west for a time above the Middle Fork of Salt Creek Valley before it turns southwest, passing the Mt. Zion Church and entering one of the few fertile valleys in the county. The terrain changes, the roadside becomes more scenic as the road nears Story.

STORY

Tale of a Town

Motorists have no choice, but to stop in Story. A stop sign—where Ind. 135 meets a county road—demands it.

A sign welcomes motorists to "Historic Story." Except for old buildings and some items from earlier eras there is nothing to substantiate the "historic" claim.

No matter! Story has become a popular destination for dining and lodging at the Story Inn, part of which occupies what once was an old general store where gas pumps—for Royal Crown and Red Crown gasoline—remain.

A house next door is called the "Blue Lady." A yellow home with gray trimming and a rail fence out front is on the "Village Green." An old dump hay rake and two running gears of ancient farm wagons are in the yard.

Imagination has turned a village that was on sale for $40,000 in the early 1960s into a viable business.

*   *   *

Ind. 135 makes an abrupt direction change from southwest to southeast at the stop sign in Story. It will not be the last sharp deviation for turns on the road ahead are frequent.

SPURGEON'S CORNER

One-Stop Town

A town could not be more aptly named than Spurgeon's Corner. It is on the corner of Ind. 135 at Beck's Grove Road in southern Brown County.

Actually it is more of a location than a town. Spurgeon's Corner Grocery on the inside southwest corner is the only business, the only building, in fact.

This is country, south central Indiana country, out where the spaces are wide and the homes are few. The nearest town is Freetown, a hamlet of 600 residents which seems large in comparison to Spurgeon's Corner.

The store, "since 1937," a promotional T-shirt boasts, is a place to stop for gasoline, food, feed, farm fresh eggs, milk, bologna, rental movies and pizza. Or varied merchandise such as pet food, magazines, lamps, hats and other items.

The building's history is older than the store. It once was, we learned on an earlier visit, a one-room school in Story. It was taken apart, board by board, and rebuilt by Jason Greathouse, whose family lived in the small upstairs while he owned the store.

*   *   *

Ind. 135 turns south at Spurgeon's Corner and runs straight for one of the few times on its route through Brown County.

A nice view appears on the vista near McKinney Cemetery Road, a prelude to fall colors that will appear in an arc across the horizon to the south on a ridge over a branch of Salt Creek. A mile ahead, Brown County ends, Jackson County begins.

The road no longer is straight. Atop a rise, a sign notes the location of Noe School - 1870-1923. It is a memento from an era when students walked or rode horses or "hacks" to what parents called "common" schools. Most such schools have long been forgotten. The foresight of those who posted the marker has kept Noe a part of the area's legacy.

A stone's throw away, a county road leads off Ind. 135 two mile southwest to Houston, where its old high school is being preserved.

Ind. 135 continues its slithering route south, speed limits set as low as 15 mph for some hairpin turns. The road follows Kiper Creek as it approaches Freetown past a new Church of Christ. (See Freetown in Ind. 58 section).

Ind. 58 joins Ind. 135 at the west edge of Freetown, then departs on its route 1.5 miles to the south. Ind. 135 continues its sinuous route for three miles before heading due south through the White River bottoms to U.S. 50.

The road joins U.S. 50, crosses White River and enters the west edge of Brownstown where it resumes its destination south to the Ohio River.

BROWNSTOWN

Home Grown

Downtown Brownstown is a mile from Ind. 135 but it is worth a detour. It is neat, clean, a county seat town of 2,978 residents that seems idyllic compared to major cities and overrun suburban communities.

It remains like a small town of the mid-1950s, little changed by time. Except for a McDonald's, there are few franchise operations.

Much of the conversation centers around the Brownstown Central High School athletic teams, where the football team is usually ranked among the best in its class and the girls athletic squads often dominate conference play.

The heart of the town is Courthouse Square, ringed by a wrought iron fence; the two-story buff brick Courthouse topped by a tower with a clock. A historical marker memorializes Col. John Ketcham (1782-1865) "fearless pioneer, ranger, surveyor, public servant," who dedicated the square for the seat of government of Jackson County when Brownstown was founded in 1816. A granite memorial to veterans is near the marker.

Across U.S. 50 from the courthouse are old store buildings, two and three stories, identified by engravings of names such as Fassold & Block and Wright-Vermilya. Most of the buildings remain occupied, at least on the lower level, for this is still a trading center for area residents.

To the north is Brownstown Feed & Supply, which reflects the rural nature of the town where prize watermelons are grown in the sands of the East Fork of White River. It is the Watermelon Festival, featuring one of the state's better parades, that brings hundreds of visitors to the town each September.

An old livery stable off the square is the center for the Jackson County Historical Society. Its many mementos include relics of the days when horsepower came from horses not from giant farm tractors and high-speed cars.

Visitors, who are in the area in the fall when leaves turn into a myriad of colors, are advised to take a detour to Skyline Drive.

The narrow three-mile paved road is a series of sharp turns, each turn a prelude to spectacular beauty. To the north is a postcard view of Brownstown, to the south a panorama of the Starve Hollow Lake area.

At their peak, the leaves become nature's masterpiece, a canvas of colors, a creation of nature too good to share, yet too good to keep from others.

*   *   *

Ind. 135 heads south from U.S. 50 and—chocolate lovers beware—soon passes a factory outlet for Russell Stover Candies. To the south toward Vallonia a sign notes the area where a soldier attached to nearby Fort Vallonia was attacked during an Indian ambush in October, 1812.

Ahead, Main Street leads off the state highway into the heart of Vallonia.

VALLONIA

War and Peace

Almost every town claims it is "historic." Vallonia has proof it was a pioneer settlement before Indiana became a state.

A fort, on what was an Indian trail, dates back to the 1810s. Known as Fort Vallonia, the stockade was built as a stockade for the protection of early settlers, then was used in the War of 1812 by Maj. John Tipton and his garrison.

Now restored, walls of wood give it an appearance of authenticity. Not far away a sign marks a "Treaty Elm," the site of an 1813 peace treaty signed by Shawnee Indian chiefs.

These events are remembered when Fort Vallonia Days bring thousands of visitors to the unincorporated town each year on the third October weekend. Proceeds help maintain the fort and the Fort Vallonia Museum on Main Street.

Main Street leads through the heart of the old town, where the post office appears to be the newest structure. The 1914 Jackson Hotel, a roof extending from its first floor over the sidewalk, is due for restoration.

Sign promotes Fort Vallonia

Little changed by time is the Bluebird Café, where owner Doris Wheeler has served meals and drinks for almost 60 years. She and her late husband, Dan, bought the place in 1944 when a beer sold for 15 cents, and men too old to fight talked about the war that raged in Europe and the Pacific.

It's a typical small town hangout where men enter as strangers and leave as friends.

The high school gym, once the home of the Vallonia Redbirds, remains, a block away, although students have attended Brownstown Central since 1962. Mention basketball in town and an old-timer is certain to recall coach Hubert Bastin's 1950 team that was among the Final 32 teams in the state tournament.

Vallonia, however is known for more than its fort, its annual festival and basketball. It's known for recreation. Southeast of town is Starve Hollow, a state recreation area with a 145-acre lake that is a popular retreat for fishing and swimming. The view from the dam is splendid on a fall day when the leaves coat the horizon with color.

The Vallonia State Tree Nursery and Driftwood State Fish Hatchery also are in the area.

*   *   *

Ind. 135 arcs to the east around Vallonia, then continues south through bottom land where the sand is ideal for watermelons, a cash crop for farmers.

A mile south of Vallonia, Ind. 235 begins its four-mile route to Medora, a river town of 565 residents.

A marker to the south on Ind. 135 notes the location of Driftwood Church, the first congregation in Jackson County. The log church opened in 1816 to "all denominations of orderly Christians" as a part of the Silver Creek Baptist Association. It was reorganized as a Christian Church in 1839 and later moved across the road where it remains in updated facilities.

A round barn, one of a number in the area, is near the church. A tree-covered range rises to the south as we approach the Muscatatuck River, which divides Jackson and Washington Counties.

Off to the west is the old river community of Millport. Only scattered houses remain, but a sign announces that Hamlin's Millport Store is "opening soon" in a stone building.

At the Muscatatuck, Ind. 135 begins a two-mile incline. The Knobstone Trail, popular with hikers, begins near the crest of the ridge. The elevation gives those who scan the horizon a sense of being atop the world, the heavens only miles above.

At a farm nearby a house, barn and other buildings have green roofs and brown siding trimmed in white. A black wooden fence encloses the grounds.

A few miles south is Kossuth, a rural community with a greenhouse, a cemetery, a few houses and a concrete building that appears to be vacant. Salem is seven miles to the south, the road is straight but seldom flat.

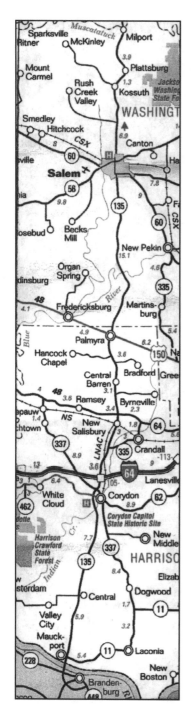

SALEM

Often Overlooked

Old, well-maintained homes line Ind. 135 which enters Salem as Main Street. It is a city seldom mentioned in the Indianapolis media or in state tourism promotions, but it is worth a visit.

The city's core is the 1888 Washington County Courthouse, which sets on a square in the path of Main Street where traffic is diverted on a circular pattern.

Locally-quarried limestone was used to erect the Richardsonian Romanesque style courthouse with a clock on its tower.

On display on the first floor are items from the past and information about the county and its history that began in 1814. A marker outside notes July 10, 1864, Salem's date of infamy. It was the day Confederate Gen. John Hunt Morgan and his raiders took over the town, destroyed the depot and cut telegraph lines before departing as quickly as they arrived.

A memorial to area residents who have died in wars is on the southeast corner of the square. All those who have served are remembered on the diagonal corner with a verse:

> *"Let none forget they gave their all,*
> *"And faltered not when came the call."*

Most of the storefronts around the square are occupied with stores and businesses, for Salem remains a shopping destination. The city of 6,172 residents is the largest in the area midway between Bedford, Seymour and Louisville.

Among the stores is the Sweetie Pie's Pie Company, its products made with "fresh eggs and real butter."

Another place for a taste of Salem is the Dinner Bell, a tiny café that has been a fixture for decades at 305 South Main. Lois and Jesse Powell ran the operation from 1958 to 2001 when it was sold.

Men—and some women—who stop at the café daily hope the new owners will carry on the Powell tradition as they indicated they would.

Small, narrow and cramped with just enough stools and tables to seat 27 diners, it offers a view of Americana that has almost faded into history.

Eggs sizzle on the grill behind the counter where men come day after day for coffee, breakfast and to share their lives, their stories and their jokes.

It's far different than the impersonal Wendy's and McDonald's that are along Ind. 135 as it winds its way south out of town.

A good time to visit Salem is in September when Old Settlers Days features a juried arts and craft exhibit, food, entertainment, pioneer demonstrations and storytelling around a campfire. Another attraction is the John Hay Center, which includes the Stevens Memorial Museum and the Pioneer Village.

*   *   *

South of Salem, narrow bridges span small creeks with soapstone bottoms as the road ripples and waves over hills and into dips.

The deviations of the road, aside, this is a scenic route, typical of southern Indiana, where the terrain changes mile by mile. It is 15 miles from Salem to Palmyra.

A historical marker at Lick Skillet Road notes the southern boundary of the Illinoian glacier, which covered all but 6,250 square miles of south central Indiana a million years ago. Most of the state's typography, the sign notes, was affected by four separate glacier advancements during the Pleistocene epoch.

Small farms, wooded hills and a few rural homes are on the route that crosses a branch of Blue River five miles north of the Washington-Harrison County line.

Nice homes on big lots line the road as Ind. 135 eases south, then crosses U.S. 150 in the town of Palmyra.

PALMYRA
Trail Blazing

Palmyra began as "Cross Roads" and continues to exist as a community built around the two highways.

U.S. 150 began as the Vincennes Trail, which stretched across southern Indiana from the Ohio west to Vincennes, the capital of the Indiana Territory. Ind. 135 started as a trail carved by early travelers north from the Ohio River.

The two roads met in Cross Roads, believed to be the first intersection in the state. "Cross Roads" became a settlement in 1808. It later was known as Carthage, then became Palmyra, the name of King Solomon's city in Syria.

Hays McCallan bought much of the land that became Palmyra in 1810 and built the first post office and a hotel, which likely was an overnight stop when the Vincennes Trail became a stagecoach route a decade later.

The Palmyra of the 21st Century has a town government, 633 residents, a few businesses along U.S. 150 and a history that is older than the state.

*   *   *

South of Palmyra, the farm fields are small in this area deep in southern Indiana, far from the prairies to the north.

Off Ind. 135 to the west is Morgan Elementary School, which doubled as a high school for Palmyra and other township villages until 1969 when consolidated North Harrison High opened.

Ahead is Central Barren, a community that stretches like a shoe string along Ind. 135.

It is known today only by its name on the highway sign for little remains of its past that dates back to the early 1800s when the famed Buffalo Trace ran through the area. Often called

Indiana's first highway, the trace connected Clarksville on the Ohio River to Vincennes on the Wabash River.

Bradford Road leads east from Charity Baptist Church in Central Barren. In ecumenical unity, a sign for St. Michael's Catholic Church in Bradford is posted on the Baptist Church lawn.

Bradford is home to the Gettelfinger Popcorn Company, the impressive St. Michael's Church and the Bradford Tavern. Lawns of almost half the homes in the small town display the Ten Commandments.

NEW SASLISBURY

Another Crossroads

At first glance, New Salisbury looks like a Palmyra rerun. It, too, begins at an Ind. 135 crossroads, this one with Ind. 64, which runs across southern Indiana.

A new bank is at a corner of the intersection and most of the businesses are on the east-west road. The post office, closed at noon for lunch, is to the south on Ind. 135.

Off to the west is the old New Salisbury High School, once the home of the Tigers. The school now is divided into apartments and students attend North Harrison High out on Ind. 64.

New Salisbury remains unincorporated, its government managed by Harrison County office holders.

It is, however, in an area that could boom soon as metropolitan Louisville continues to mushroom to the northwest.

*   *   *

A golf course is south of town near an intersection with Ind. 335, which leads east to Crandall. A sign on a corner of the junction reads "Emilyville USA." There is no one to ask if it is a husband's tribute to a spouse named Emily.

The old town of Corydon is just ahead past an interchange with I-64.

CORYDON

In The Beginning . . .

In reality there are two Corydons. One is the complex of restaurants, motels and shopping outlets that sprawl out on the
ridge from the Ind. 135-I-64 interchange. The other is the old
Corydon, where statehood began and history can be relived, down
in the Indian Creek valley.

Old State Capitol in downtown Corydon

Ind. 135, which once ran through the heart of old Corydon now bypasses it to the west. Businesses, that extend for two miles along the road, include a super Wal-Mart, a Cracker Barrel and fast food restaurants, convenience stores and outlets usually found in much larger towns.

That is the superficial Corydon. The real Corydon can be reached via old Ind. 135 from the north or Ind. 62 from the west. It is a detour off the bypass that should not be overlooked.

Once downtown, it is best to park the car and stroll through the pages of time recorded on historical markers and in the buildings that remain from an earlier era. It is a jewel, too good to miss for few towns are as old, as significant or as engaging.

There, too, are art and craft shops and stores operated by entrepreneurs, not managers who run chain operations at the whims of corporate officers.

Corydon's attractions are "too numerous to mention." They do, of course, include the first State Capitol, a two-story brick with an octagonal cupola at the top. Built as the Harrison County Courthouse, it served as the first state capitol from 1816 until 1825 when the center of state government was moved to Indianapolis.

Nearby on the wooded historical mall is the three-story Harrison County Courthouse built of stone in 1929.

Other attractions in the area include the first State Office Building, also known as the Old Treasury Building. It was used by the state, while the capitol was in Corydon, and is part of the Corydon Capitol State Historic Site.

Scene in downtown Corydon's business area

Old homes nearby include the residence where Gov. William Hendricks resided from 1922 to 1925, the Westfall House, which was built of logs in 1807 and the Kitner House Inn, erected in 1873 and restored in 1986.

Corydon's history didn't end when Indianapolis became the state capital. South of town is the five-acre Battle Park. It was in the area where Gen. John Morgan and his 2,000 confederate soldiers overwhelmed the local militia and volunteers in 1863. Names of both the Union and Confederate dead are listed on a monument at the site.

Off Ind. 135 south of Ind. 62 is the Hayswood Nature Reserve, a 160-acre park with hiking trails and access to Indian Creek which flows through Corydon, which is the home of Gov. Frank O'Bannon.

                         *   *   *

Ind. 135 is a wide, straight route south of Corydon as it heads for Mauckport and the Ohio River. A few businesses and farms are on the seven-mile drive to the community of Central.

CENTRAL
Surviving Change

Central, too, was bypassed to the west by Ind. 135, but hints of the old road remain.

Facing the old route is the Bethel United Methodist Church, where a sign promises a "Free trip to Heaven - Details Inside." Nearby is a graveyard adjacent to a patch of tobacco, a cash crop for southern Indiana farmers.

One of Indiana's general stores, the kind that served small towns across the state, remains a fixture in Central. Called Hardsaw and Longbottom, it is a supermarket for farmers looking for lumber, metal siding, roofing, fencing, feed and seed.

It is Central's main business, just as it has been since 1929 when Longbottom opened the store. The Hardsaw part came later, creating a name that has survived all competitors.

Clark Hardsaw, grandson of a Longbottom, son of a Hardsaw, remains behind his desk as he has been since 1977 extending the family enterprise into the third generation.

On an earlier visit, he explained, "It's the same type of operation it has been for years. It's the same store, except there are even fewer farmers," he says, this being an era when farms grow larger in size, farmers fewer in number.

One thing has changed. The county health department shut down the meat counter, which had been in the store for 49 years. It claimed the sink was too far from the meat counter. Bureaucracy rules, we all know.

"The EPA took our gas pumps a few years go and the health department got our meat counter. The government is gradually taking the old general stores down," he adds.

Across the road from the store are its farm building supplies, the metal barn sales and the portable toilet and septic business. It's a big operation, one general store operators of a half-century ago would have envied.

*   *   *

A view of the horizon is limitless as Ind. 135 continues over the six miles to the Ohio River.

Off the road are the Squire Boone Caverns, a privately-owned attraction with a cave featuring a column that rises almost 50 feet. A ramp onto Ind. 11 leads to the oft-flooded town of Mauckport.

MAUCKPORT

By the Riverside

A 12 percent population decline seems like a lot of people. Not here where the census showed a loss of 12—from 95 to 83—between 1990 to 2000.

Life has never been easy here on the river. Floods have devastated the town, testing the mettle of its people, forcing some to move on, others to stay and rebuild their lives and their homes. The worst disaster came in 1937, when the destruction threatened to end Mauckport as a community.

It survived, but, like some other river towns, it was never the same.

Expectations of a rebirth came in the 1990s when a marina, which was to feature a yacht club, loading dock, tennis court and club house, was planned. It never developed. Another setback came when a riverboat casino was located upriver nearer Louisville.

Credit John Peter Mauck for the town's existence. He obtained the area through a land grant and opened the first ferry into Indiana from Kentucky that became a passage to the Northwest. Settlers could travel the 17 miles from Mauckport to Corydon on a route now taken by Ind. 135.

The town soon became a busy river port and a home here an underground railroad station. That could be why Gen. John Morgan and his raiders lobbed a shot through the house from across the river at Brandenburg, Kentucky. The shot was a prelude to their incursion into Indiana during the Civil War.

Few businesses remain in Mauckport where the post office, its operation a family affair for six decades, is a community center of sorts. Postmaster Linnea Dean Breeden grew up in town and knows almost everyone around the area. Her father, Welton Dean, was Postmaster for ten years (1945 to 1956). He was followed by her mother, Kathryn Dean Timberlake, who had the job for 30 years before she was succeeded by Linnea.

An annual event is the Mauckport River Fest held the second weekend in August.

Ind. 135 and the state boundary end where the Matthew Welsh Bridge crosses the Ohio River. The span, which opened in 1966, was named for Welsh, Indiana's governor in the 1960s.

*   *   *

The road, which started in Indianapolis, has passed through the burgeoning suburbs of Johnson County, bisected rich farm land, crossed the beauty of Brown County, seen the sandy bottoms of White River, and traveled the rollercoaster terrain of southern Indiana.

It is a route traveled by many of our ancestors as they moved north to develop a new state that would be called Indiana.

INDIANA 229

From U.S. 52 to Ind. 48
Curvaceously Attractive

Choose a passenger seat if you have a choice for the ten mile cruise between U.S. 52 and Ind. 48. The 21-mile route offers great vistas . . . unless you are the driver, who is occupied with the constant curves.

Few roads are as winding or as scenic as the northern section of this route. Warning signs for twists are common, limiting speeds to 15, 20, 25 mph. Sharp turns, 90-degree at times, are numerous. An open space now and then allows a speed of 40 mph, but only for a short distance.

* * *

Ind. 229 begins at U.S. 52 a mile west of Metamora, a tourist town with an old mill on what once was the Whitewater Canal. The meandering road leaves the valley, coils up an incline as it heads south. Homes are common, their owners seeking retreats from towns and cities on affordable sites that offer tranquillity amid scenic settings.

Five miles from U.S. 52, the road rises into Peppertown.

PEPPERTOWN
Scenery and Spice

A two-story building, walled with native stone from area quarries, has been restored. It is just one of the stone structures that reflect the stone craftsmanship of an earlier time.

The hamlet, platted in 1859, owes its name to August Pepper, a German immigrant and shopkeeper. The German influence remains for there is a Lutheran Church but no other congregations.

An old store has been converted to a residence, as has a brick school. An old cemetery is on both sides of a county road at the edge of town. Like all rural graveyards it welcomes and appreciates donations to pay mowing and other expenses.

There are no stores, no businesses in Peppertown.

*   *   *

Just south of Peppertown, a Franklin County rural road leads east to isolated Oak Forest, a community with a general store. Residents in the area call Oak Forest "the boondocks," but, for those who have time to make the detour, it is an interesting diversion from urban Indiana.

Back on Ind. 229, the road appears to follow a ridge south, past rolling farms off to the sides. The views are at times panoramic, the foliage in the fall a myriad of color.

Ind. 229 becomes less winding toward Oldenburg, but a 50 mph speed is soon followed by a 30 mph warning.

OLDENBURG
A European Flavor

At a turn in the road, three spires rise majestically over the hills on which Oldenburg is built. It is indeed the "City of Spires" it calls itself.

City is a misnomer. Oldenburg in reality is a village of 647 residents that has retained its European character and its German heritage.

Named after a province in Germany, Oldenburg has a combination of stone, brick and framed homes, most of which are set on inclines.

Streets carry bilingual names, such as the German Wasserstrasse, with the English name Water under it; Weinstrasse (Washington Street), Hauptstrasse (Main Street).

Holy Family Church at Hauptstrasse and Perlenstrasse (Pearl Street) is the town's spiritual center. It was built in 1862, 25 years after the church was organized and Oldenburg was platted.

The Holy Family Parish Cemetery and the Immaculate Conception Convent Cemetery are at the north end of Pearl Street.

Across the street from Holy Family is the Immaculate Conception Convent, the motherhouse of the of the Third Order of the Sisters of St. Francis, founded by Vienna-born Mother Hackelmeier in 1851. The Franciscan Sisters serve schools, hospitals, parishes and missions.

The Oldenburg Academy for girls was founded in 1885 and now has a co-ed high school enrollment of 165 students. It is a member of the Indiana High School Athletic Association and its students participate in eight sports as the "Twisters." The school is at 1 Twister Circle.

Numerous other locations are worth noting, although Hackman's General Store, erected in 1861, ceased operation a decade or so ago.

It is a busy town, with a lumber company, a garage, stores, bank, flower shop and a pet grooming business. As with all German villages, there are taverns and restaurants such as King's Tavern, the Brau Haus and Wagner's Village Inn.

This is a town to park and walk at leisure. Streets are free of litter. Century-old buildings are well maintained. One historic site follows another. All that is needed to imagine oneself in a European setting is imagination.

The worries of the world beyond can be forgotten . . . at least for a few hours in Oldenburg.

*   *   *

The road snakes south out of Oldenburg toward Batesville, three miles ahead. En route Franklin County ends, Ripley County begins.

Ind. 229 crosses I-74 at the north edge of Batesville (see Ind. 46 chapter), continues through town, proceeds nine miles through farm country, passes the community of Ballstown and ends at Ind. 48.

*   *   *

The 15 roads in this book are just a few of Indiana's Roads Less Traveled. In subsequent volumes we hope to record the highlights of others.

Indiana is a state of contrasts, the diversity endless, the scenery ever changing. We hope you take the slow lanes, up and down, back and forth, across the state. The two-lane roads await you. Enjoy the difference from the routine of the interstates. Savor the experience.

INDEX

Other Books By Wendell Trogdon

NOSTALGIA:

Titles	Retail Price
Those Were the Days	Out of print.
Through the Seasons	$8.95
Carved in Memory	$8.95
Back Home	$8.95
The Country Bumpkin Gang	$10.45
Indiana General Stores	Out of print
Main Street Diners	$14.95

TRAVEL:

Backroads Indiana	$13.50
Borderline Indiana	$14.95
U.S. 50 - The Forgotten Highway	$14.95
Lonely is the Road - U.S. 50 Across America	$13.45

BIOGRAPHY:

Out Front: The Cladie Bailey Story	$9.50

BASKETBALL:

No Harm No Foul: Referees Are People, Too	$6.95
Basket Cases	$7.95
Gym Rats: Sons Who Play For Fathers	Out of Print
Shooting Stars: Trek to a Championship	$7.95
Whistle Blowers: A No Harm/No Foul Sequel.	$7.95
Damon - Living A Dream (with Damon Bailey)	$14.95

For more information about any of these books, contact the author at P.O. Box 651, Mooresville, IN 46158-0651, call him at 317-831-2815, or send an e-mail message to wend@iquest.net.

ABOUT THE AUTHOR

Indiana At Random is author Wendell Trogdon's 19th book.

Five of those books are vignettes of his experiences as a farm youth in rural southern Indiana in the 1930s and 1940s.

Five others are about Indiana high school basketball as seen from the viewpoint of referees, coaches and fans. He was co-author of a sixth basketball book, *Damon-Living A Dream*, a review of Damon Bailey's life as an Indiana legend.

Some of his most popular books have been about roads: *Backroads Indiana*, a journal of his travels over unbeaten paths to small southern Indiana towns; *Borderline Indiana*, a look at the people and places on the borders of the state; *U.S. 50: From Washington to St. Louis*, and *Lonely is the Road - U.S. 50 from St. Louis to Sacramento*.

Among his other titles are *Indiana General Stores/Vanishing Landmarks*, and *Main Street Diners/Where Hoosiers Start The Day*.

Trogdon retired as managing editor of *The Indianapolis News* in 1992 after a 38-year career that began as a reporter for the *Logansport Pharos-Tribune*. He has continued to write for other periodicals.

He resides at Mooresville, Indiana, with his wife Fabian, who traveled with him on his journeys over most of the roads covered in this book.

The author may be reached at P.O. Box 651, Mooresville, IN 46158-0651. He may be contacted by e-mail at wend@iquest.net or by phone at 317-831-2815.